GARY WILTSHIRE

FIFTY YEARS IN THE BETTING JUNGLE

All rights reserved. No part of this publication may be reproduced, stored in a retrieval system, transmitted, or utilised in any form or by any means electronic, mechanical, photocopying, recording audio or visual, or otherwise, without written prior permission of the copyright owner.

Copyright © Gary Wiltshire, 2025
First published in Great Britain in 2025

ISBN 978-1-915899-08-8

The right of Gary Wiltshire to be identified as the Author of this work has been asserted by him in accordance with the Copyright, Designs and Patents Acts 1988.

A CIP catalogue record for this book is available from the British Library.

Published by Weatherbys Ltd in conjunction with Gary Wiltshire,
this book is produced entirely in the UK and is available to order from Weatherbys Shop, www.weatherbysshop.co.uk and other outlets:

Weatherbys Ltd
Sanders Road
Wellingborough
Northamptonshire
NN8 4BX
United Kingdom
www.weatherbys.co.uk

Disclaimer
Every effort has been made to ensure the accuracy of the information contained in this publication. All content provided is the responsibility of the author. The author has been advised to ensure that every effort has been made to trace or contact all copyright holders. The author has stated to the publishers that the contents of this book are true. Neither the publisher nor the author can accept responsibility for any errors or omissions, particularly where horses change ownership or trainers after the publication has gone to print. The author and publishers disclaim, as far as the law allows, any liability arising directly or indirectly from the use, or misuse, of any information contained in this book.
Any veterinary information in this book is based on the author's personal observation, research or experience and should not be relied upon as a substitute for professional advice.
The thoughts, opinions and content of this book are that of the author and do not reflect the views and opinions of Weatherbys Ltd.

DESIGNED, PRODUCED AND PUBLISHED BY WEATHERBYS

Contents

	Introduction	5
	From the Co-Author	9
	Acknowledgements	13
	Prologue	17
1.	Nice One Sirrell	29
2.	Learning My Trade	41
3.	In A Right Old Flap	57
4.	Oxford Dogs	69
5.	Getting To The Point	79
6.	Hitting The Fairways	93
7.	Owning It	101
8.	The Cheltenham Rollercoaster	115
9.	Would The Real Dick Turpin Please Stand Up?	131
10.	The Diamond From Dagenham	147
11.	The Towcester Files	167
12.	Characters From The Betting Jungle	177
13.	Dettori Day	199
14.	These Days	213

Introduction

As far back as I can remember, I always wanted to become a bookie. Not quite as dramatic an opening line as Henry Hill in *Goodfellas* after slamming down the car trunk on the blood-spattered, mangled-up Billy Batts who his associates had just diced and sliced and Martin Scorsese has yet to get in touch but we'll give the rest of it a good bash.

Now that I have reached the distinguished age of seventy, which many of you will have regarded as around a 10/1 poke given my self-imposed health issues and colourful life story, as 2025 will mark fifty years since I first started out in the game as a clerk at Milton Keynes dogs, what better landmark to look back on the best and the worst of my rollercoaster career in a 'warts and all' look back at my time in the betting jungle? You might think that I look like a sweet and innocent baby-faced cherub but as you will discover I didn't always act like an angel.

Since *Winning It Back* was published 14 years ago, an autobiography of which a large part naturally focussed on Dettori Day, so much has changed in my life. Therefore, in addition to spilling the beans about my personal betting-ring tales, as well as wanting to bring back to life the characters, smells and give a sense of what the energy of the betting jungle used to be all about, I think it's important to begin by updating those of you who kindly took time out to read my first book about my subsequent five D's; Divorce, Depression, Diet, Diabetes and Done (Fred) so I have devoted the opening section to that before moving onto what you might describe as the jucier stuff.

In fact, make that the six D's as the Dettori story still follows me around wherever I go almost thirty years later so of course I can't not mention it again. What Greatest Hits compilation doesn't include its banger with a remastered version? Unlike in *Winning It Back* though, it's just one chapter rather than a meaty portion of the book. It's the story that made me... and some would say that I have been living off for three decades since. And they would be 100% right! It's incredible, almost every day and everywhere I go.

They should make a film about it. In fact, it has been floated with Ray Winstone playing yours truly. He would need some extra padding, though. Will it ever get off the ground? Who knows? But after losing £1.4 million (around £3 million today) on one race at Ascot with just £2,000 in my back pocket, I eventually got back off the ground even if it took me four years to pay it all back. Where and how I was brought up alongside villains like Jack Spot, Albert Dimes and The Krays, whose mother was a regular at my parents' flower stall in Leather Lane, you paid! It was as simple as that! For honour as much as anything else because if you haven't got your name and reputation in this game, then you have got nothing.

I certainly wouldn't be writing this book had it not been for Frankie's 'Magnificent Seven'. Ironically, I am told that number one in the charts that week was *Ready Or Not (here I come)* by The Fugees. It's fair to say that I certainly was not ready for what was about to come that fateful day! If you want the full SP then I am sure that you can find a copy of *Winning It Back* for around a fiver if you scour around the internet and there are certainly a good few interviews on *YouTube* about it. Fujiyama Crest's SP was 2/1 by the way despite being a genuine 16/1 chance. Just saying!

I hope that regaling some of my better-known and very much less-well-known experiences from a wide range of events that you can punt on, with a handful of others not involving me thrown in, will not just entertain you but also take you back to the good old days where the betting jungle was the beating heart of the racecourse or "a seething mass of greed and humanity" as John McCririck coined it at the beginning of one Cheltenham Festival.

Glamourous and grubby in equal measure, maybe a bit more on the grubby side if I am being truthful but I wouldn't have wanted it any other way, the betting ring is where rich and poor rubbed shoulders, bringing together people from all walks of life.

So, you can keep your Las Vegas casinos and your stock market exchange trading floors as for me there was no place like the betting ring on a busy racecourse in its heyday, feeling that electricity and looking into the whites of each other eyes when taking a bet rather than the faceless keyboard players of today taking out all of the romance.

Be kind, be generous but, most of all, be lucky!

Gary Wiltshire

From the Co-Author

Paul Jones

I was somewhat taken aback when Gary asked me if I would assist him in putting together his follow-up book to *Winning It Back* which did so well back in 2011 as it had been over twenty years earlier when we last worked together on what was then gg.com, myself as the editor and Gary as a columnist.

So, I asked him why did he feel the need for another autobiography? "Oh no, it's not another autobiography, son (I'm 55). I've got so many stories from the betting ring it's unbelievable and I want to tell them."

For someone like myself who is more nostalgic than most when it comes to horseracing and misses the halcyon days when the hustle and bustle of the ring was an intrinsic element of the race day experience, with Gary having led such an extraordinarily-colourful life, wanting to be transported back in time it didn't take me long to decide that I was all-in and this was an opportunity that I could not let pass up.

But thanks, Gary, for giving me just six weeks' notice and during my busiest time of the year before you wanted it published! An impulsive decision on his part. I wonder if he made any more of those earlier in his life?

My first association with Gary was at a point-to-point in Mollington, Oxfordshire, which is notable by its incredibly stiff finish (think Towcester on steroids), back in 1987 so not long after I had turned eighteen and finally legally allowed to bet.

Back in those days only one bookie was allowed to display an unorthodox betting board in that they could price up races for forecasts or betting without the favourite etc. The Men's and Women's Opens regularly produced long odds-on favourites so I often found myself heading to Gary's pitch at the many Midlands and East Anglia courses looking for a different betting angle as he had been awarded that right. When I did bet with him during that period of five years, rather than handing me a betting ticket, he always told his clerk: "Just put that one down to 'The Boy'." So, he knew back then how to build a rapport with his clients. When I asked for the next price up with my fiver or tenner, he said I could have it for my cheek.

It was over a decade later when our paths crossed again. Looking for columnists for the launch of the GG website which was based on Easton Neston Estate including Towcester Racecourse, as Gary lived locally and was present at every meeting, he was an ideal fit to ask to write betting-based articles, also being one of the most recognisable faces (and waistlines) on British racecourses. I say 'write', he talked, fast and plenty, I wrote and shaped. Some things don't change another two decades on, I guess.

As part of the GG days, we held a Cheltenham Festival Preview Evening at the racecourse involving some of the columnists and it was in the Indian restaurant that followed in Stoke Bruerne on the canal when I first truly learned of Gary's culinary requirements. It's fair to say that I have never seen before or after anyone order and eat three curries on their own. As we learned on that infamous Dettori Day, he was one of Britain's biggest gamblers in more ways than one.

I very much enjoyed all aspects of helping Gary with this project and hope that you have as much pleasure reading it as I had piecing it together. It really was a case of what do we leave out rather than what do we put in. Now a septuagenarian, Gary remains a workaholic having had that knocked into him from an early age from his market trader days and is still a regular face in many betting arenas. One thing is for certain, the betting jungles of racecourses, greyhound tracks, point-to-points, flapping tracks, Arab race meetings, darts and snooker arenas, fishing lakes and the like would be a lot poorer without his larger-than-life presence.

***

Paul worked for Weatherbys straight from school between 1987-2001 working in various departments from production to marketing, including as a sub-editor of *Raceform* and *Chaseform*, the official Form Books and went on to be the originator, researcher and author of the *Cheltenham Festival Betting Guide* between 2000-2015 amongst other similar titles, which is still going strong over a quarter of century later.

The editor for the launch of *gg.com* in 2001 and trends analyst for *Attheraces.com* since 2003 to the current day, Paul has been running his own website *pauljoneshorseracing.com* since 2015 focussing primarily on jumps racing and is the author of his self-published, betting-related publication from 2018, *From Soba To Moldova*.

In the years between working for Weatherbys/GG and setting up his website, Paul was a form guide writer for 17 racecourses under many pseudonyms, a William Hill Radio pundit off and on for eight years and Master of Ceremonies at Towcester Racecourse between 2005-2009.

Outside of horseracing, in the last three years Paul assisted his father to write his life story shortly before his passing at the age of 89 to be given away at his funeral as a lasting memory, off the back of which he has co-written two more private autobiographies. *Fifty Years In The Betting Jungle* is the first book that he has co-written as a commercial venture in this respect and his fortieth book all told.

A music as well as horseracing devotee, Paul has become as well known in some circles for his Eurovision Song Contest betting-related content as much as his horseracing!

Acknowledgements

In the pages that follow I make reference to family and great friends and colleagues who stood by me during my darkest days but there are others who I also want to mention and give my heartfelt thanks to.

My driver Lofty, chauffeur is way too posh a description for him, has been transporting me up and down the country for over thirty years having been ITV sports presenter Gary Newbon's driver previously. We have fallen out a million times but we always make it up. Lewis Hamilton he is not but he gets me from A to B on time and is never late. My thanks also to Gary for showing me the ropes behind the mic.

Alan Ballard has been a very close friend of mine for over thirty years. We are almost like brothers. We started out together at Ladbrokes as board markers and went on to own horses together. Throughout the last fifty years he has always been someone that I can rely on.

Curly, aka Jeffrey Curry, keeps me going every day with morning calls coming out with old stories taking me back so he always puts a smile on my face.

Dermot Cumiskey for giving me a chance to appear on BBC with some of the biggest names in the sport like Willie Carson, Clare Balding and Aussie Jim McGrath amongst others. I'll never forget that. When he put a cockney and scouser together in the betting ring, many said that there was no way it would work but I thought myself and John Parrott bounced off each other really well. No pun intended!

I was a bit wary of Irish Dave (Reynolds) at first who appears in all the old London gangster books but he has turned out to be one of my closest pals and has horses with Stuart Williams amongst other trainers.

The loudest man on the course though is The Vossman and, Jamie, although you give us a blinding headache every time we see you, we love you and you bring life to the race track.

One of my oldest pals is Peter Collier who I knew from way back in my market street days and he is always seen at the races.

When I see Alan Brazil at the races, he's got time for one and all and that includes at Higham point-to-point where you can usually find him in the beer tent. Everyone loves Big Al.

Also, a massive thank you to my doctor Paul McNally who has somehow kept me going for these last few years and still keeps getting on at me when I step out of line.

If you are ever in Great Yarmouth, then have a night opposite the pier in the Greek restaurant *Othello's* where the owner, Michael, has become a real good friend of ours. Don't miss out and thank me later.

Mark Dixon is Norfolk's No. 1 chef and his lobster thermidor is to die for at the *Kings Arms* in Fleggburgh. I should write my own Best Restaurant book next! Gary's Gastronomic Guide!

Apart from a chiselled jaw line, what else do I and David Beckham have in common? Our favourite eatery is *Tony's Pie & Mash* shop in Waltham Abbey that also specialises in jellied and hot eels. Proper nosh. Becks still gets it shipped over to Los Angeles when he's based out in the States. I don't know what Posh Spice eats. Not a lot by the look of her.

And, of course, a big thank you to everyone who has bet with me over the last fifty years because without you I wouldn't be here. Win, lose or draw, we always have a smile.

Prologue

I realised that the final straw working for the Beeb came at Royal Ascot on the hottest day of the year, which was even more of a nightmare for someone of my size being forced to wear all the fancy regalia for the cameras; shirt, tie, waistcoat, jacket and topper. I have never sweated so much or been as uncomfortable in all my life.

Before racing each day, we had a morning meeting in the production van but that was about three furlongs from the betting ring and there was absolutely no way that I could physically manage to get there on foot in the heat so I bunged the car park attendant a few quid to give me a ride on his golf buggy. Part of the route was the same as for the Royal procession under the stand so I used to wave at people as I went by.

I was kitted out beforehand by *John Banks Big & Tall* in Birmingham as, being 37 stone with a 66-inch waste, there were not too many of those hanging on the peg in *Next*. It arrived at the hotel in Bracknell where the BBC staff were put up for the week in the nick of time very late on the Monday night and thankfully it fitted.

Come the fifth and final day of the meeting, when I took my jacket off the water just fell off me like I was having a shower and it was only then when it truly dawned on me that I couldn't carry on in the job. When I let them know, I didn't tell the BBC exactly why as it was too embarrassing so I made something up about still working with the Tote.

I already knew just how bad shape I was in but this was a warning shot across the bows as I had never felt as close to death than I had out there on the hot days. What's more, the racing was being shown live so it wouldn't have made the best afternoon TV if I was going to collapse and pop my clogs in front of the cameras like Tommy Cooper. If I was going to keel over on a racecourse, I'd much rather it was Great Yarmouth, which is handily on the doorstep of the James Paget Hospital!

***

It was after returning from a night meeting working for Sky Sports at Sunderland dogs that I was admitted into Solihull Hospital at about 2am.

I had guzzled down 24 bottles of Lucozade on the drive back to help with sugar levels for my diabetes and felt like I was at death's door, much worse than at Royal Ascot. With Lofty at the wheel, we were stopping at every service station and layby on the A1 to relieve myself as I was pissing just as fast as I was consuming. It was a miracle that he got me there alive as they put a drip on me as soon as I was admitted.

Word soon got round that I was in a very bad way and, unbeknown to me, who should get on the phone to my Nicky but none other than Fred Done who asked just how serious it was? My son didn't pull any wool over his eyes and gave it to him straight. Dad was in big trouble.

The following day the ward sister came to my bedside and informed me that a private ambulance had been ordered that would be arriving in half an hour to take me to Spire Parkway, a private hospital which was also in Solihull, to have a gastric sleeve operation which had already been paid for. I knew that I couldn't afford it so asked who had sorted it? She went away to check and returned a few minutes later: "A Mr Fred Done."

Well, if I wasn't already laying flat on my back then you could have knocked me down with a feather as I had only spoken to him once before in my entire life and that was seventeen years earlier after Dettori Day!

That news perked me up no end but I still knew that this was only the start as for someone of my size the surgery came with risks. Once at the Parkway, the operation was booked in for early the next morning so I had a restless night. Given my weight they needed three porters to lift me onto the trolley which then proved to be too small so I had to walk to the operating theatre. Strange things were going through my mind on the way like, what would happen about an ante-post ticket I had on the Premier League if I didn't get through it?

Once in the theatre I then noticed that the anaesthetist had a Spurs logo on his arm. As a Gooner, I said to him: "Please God don't let that be the last thing I ever see!" He reassured me that it wouldn't be and told me to keep calm and that: "You're just going for a little sleep." That's what they all tell you but what they are really doing is setting you into a coma with no pain and no dreams.

The irreversible five hours' operation involved taking out 80% of my stomach which would see my weight eventually drop from 37 stone to 23 stone and would lessen the appetite and make me feel fuller much quicker.

A day after the op the surgeon from Newcastle came to see me to show me the broken instruments that he used. They were practically destroyed. In fact, he told me that half-way through he wanted to stop and put in a balloon instead. However, I had stressed beforehand that I wanted the sleeve and had to sign forms to that effect given how dangerous the op was for someone of my size.

He also revealed that he didn't want to say anything to me beforehand but rated my chances of not coming through the operation at around 25% and that other surgeons had turned me down as it wouldn't look good on their CV having somebody croak on their operating table. A bloody good job he didn't mention it beforehand as I'd seen hundreds of 3s ON chances get turned over down the years! Mind you, I'd still rather have taken them odds over what I would have been to survive the next few weeks without Fred's intervention. I am sure that if I didn't have that op then I would have been brown bread.

***

So, what more can I say about Fred? I can state that hand on heart I had gone beyond the point of no return until he dragged me back. The day he rang up Nicky was the day that completely changed my life.

I class him as a second father and a loyal friend. He even gave me his personal phone number which he essentially only uses for family as wanted to be there 24/7 in case I fell off the precipice again but I'm not going for the hat-trick anytime soon! I can never repay you enough, old chum. Great men rarely enter one's life and Fred is certainly that.

Naturally, when I survived the operation the first thing that I wanted to do was thank Fred for his incredible generosity and saving me. During that conversation he told me that when I was fit again to come and appear on Betfred TV in Birchwood, where the studios were at the time. They have since moved to Media City in Salford where the

BBC is also based only around a mile away from Fred's first shop, so to all intents and purposes he was heading back home.

The first time I met Fred in the flesh was for a Saturday morning show which he still appears on today. When I clapped my eyes on him, I burst into tears and hugged him. There are no airs and graces about Fred, he was one of 'us' who had made it big. A man of the people. He is also a big Manchester United fan but we all have our crosses to bear.

So we struck up an immediate rapport and he always invited me to his annual party at the Hilton Hotel in Manchester where no expense was spared whatsoever. Kylie Minogue to name but one. I'll leave it at that.

'Fred's Pushes' are fantastic for betting shop punters where he lengthens the odds on four or five favourites on Saturday mornings. He'd ask the presenter Geordie Paul: "What are we going on this favourite?" 7/4. "What's the best price in the village?" 7/4. "No scrub that, 5/2 for the next thirty minutes." He doesn't care if they win, in fact he wants them to win as he told me: "Offer them something they can't get elsewhere and they will bet with me for life." True, that.

His brilliant head of media is Mark Pearson who always makes me feel very welcome but I had just one request when we worked in Birchwood, could he upgrade the stairs to an elevator please? No worries on that score now as there are three lifts up to the ninth floor.

Fred's dad used to take bets through a hole in his garden gate under the name of Fred Hyde as he lived in Hyde Street in Salford so he was the original back-street bookmaker.

Fred started his bookmaking career in 1967 when alongside his brother Peter they opened up their first shop in Ordsall, Salford. The previous year they had backed England big to win the World Cup which funded their venture. Today they are the number one high-street bookmaker with 1,400 betting offices in Britain in addition to the online business and owning shops in South Africa. From small acorns large oak trees grow so the saying goes.

Fred and Mo were childhood sweethearts so I can't imagine how hard it was for him when she devastatingly passed of cancer in 2018? When Fred started as a backstreet bookie, Mo was one of his runners and she would always sign the betting dockets 'Mo 21'. Honoured to be in attendance at her funeral, she was a woman I held dear to my heart and we formed a great friendship so I felt that I had to do something afterwards.

So I rang up my old pal Domimic Magnone in Ireland who could get his hands on dozens of dogs for sale and I asked him to pick out the prettiest bitch with the best temperament but on the proviso that she must be able to run. He sent me some photos of Lissatouk Snow, who was white with a few black markings and I knew straight away this was exactly what I was looking for. She had been soundly beaten in her four races at Limerick but Dom assured me that she would improve with experience and I wouldn't have approached him in the first place if I didn't respect his judgement.

Once she was settled into the Lancashire kennels of Pat Rosney and his partner Julie McCombe, we renamed her Mo Twentyone.

After we sat down together and watched her four races on DVD, they were both of the opinion that she was, in fact, useless. I told them to let me worry about that as I had faith in Dom and then in her first trial at Belle Vue, she proved him right and Pat and Julie wrong, which they were very happy to be. She passed the grading time easily so only then did I feel comfortable to inform Fred that I had bought them a dog registered under the name of 'Mo's Family and Friends' Syndicate'.

Fred's daughter Leanne asked me: "Why are you doing all this, Gary, it's fantastic?" The answer was very simple: "Your mum and dad saved my life." I'd been holding myself together really well until then but the waterworks then came on like sprinklers. It had been such a privilege to give something back.

Mo Twentyone did indeed progress physically throughout the summer just as Dom had anticipated and she hit gold on her third start for the syndicate at Belle Vue in front of the whole family who collected the trophy. She was quietly fancied at 9/4 and came home in good style looking a real, nice prospect.

The following day Fred took some of his family including the grandkids over to visit her at Leyland Kennels in her home surroundings where they all got on so famously that Fred retired her on the spot to take her home as a pet.

***

Back to when I was dead to the world in the operating theatre, my second wife Susan was waiting in my room and unbeknown to me had been looking through my mobile phone messages. She found a text message from my close friend Sharon wishing me all the best for the surgery and that we should meet up for lunch when you're out of hospital.

I was discharged on Valentine's Day morning so I took Susan to an Italian restaurant called *Ciello* in Brindley Place in Birmingham and had what I thought was a lovely evening. Once we got back to the house, she told me about how she had gone through my phone and accused me of playing away from home. She was putting two and two together and coming up with five. I protested my innocence and explained that weighing in at 37 stone I was hardly a catch. I was Gary Wiltshire not Gary Barlow!

I begged with her to believe me knowing nothing was untoward but she was adamant that I was up to no good. I had done a million other things that I wasn't proud of, but this wasn't one. She was deadly serious and the next morning she walked out the door and left me.

I was left shell-shocked as this had come from right out of the blue and also when I needed her most as I wasn't in any shape to look after myself and couldn't use the stairs with sixty-nine stitches under my stomach. I was also a technophobe, let alone knowing how to change a plug, and I still don't, but much more than that I just didn't do being alone.

Maybe her decision was more to do with the lifestyle that I was living? She once told a friend that when he comes through the door she didn't know if we were going to have an exotic holiday abroad or have to sell the house. Granted, it wasn't the best security so I could understand it if that was the case but not the harmless text messages. Now Susan is living with the man who was building her menage at the stables which she owned at the time when she left me.

Three days later when it was obvious that she was not coming back to me, I rented a flat in St Francis Drive in King's Norton but

I couldn't sleep there as my head was completely gone so ended up kipping in the car for the nights, only entering the flat during the day. Sleeping in cars was something that I was comfortable enough with having done so on many occasions after evening meetings travelling from racecourses up and down the land.

All of this then sent me into a deep depression which became my most difficult opponent and kept me off the racecourse for a full year. Frankie couldn't keep me away but this did. A couple of weeks after the op, I got a phone call from Sharon asking how I was getting on with my recovery so I told her absolutely everything. She told me that there was no way she could have me sleeping in a car, especially whilst in recovery, so to come and stay in her spare room in Dale Road in Keyworth to get my head down and relax properly.

She had split from her husband and was living with her teenage daughter, Jaimee. Although I was grateful for the offer, I said that it wouldn't be fair on Jaimee but Sharon was adamant. This time helped me out no end, I can't tell you.

Although there was no romance between me and Sharon, it must have been hard for Jaimee to suddenly have another man in her life but we got there in the end. She's a great girl and has occasionally worked for me on pitches since and is now a police officer and I know how proud Sharon is of her, as am I.

After six months we had moved into a nice cottage in the suburbs owned by Sharon's friend from the Pony Club which had a stream at the bottom of the garden. It also had a big greenhouse which I got to know very well as, not wanting to return to bookmaking, I would sit there for hours on end with the geraniums, petunias and tomato plants rather than suffering hours of daytime TV or the racing as just getting up was too much of an effort.

What did get me out was that Sharon needed a new runaround so I went to buy one off Champagne Charlie at Nottingham Car Centre. He basically told me that he didn't want to sell me anything until I had sorted myself out. He had been through a bad time himself but had a chance meeting with a psychoanalyst called Terry Leahy who steered him back on the right path. Charlie handed over me his card and said: "Go and see Terry and only then will I sell you a car."

I thought what harm could it do seeing a shrink and even just talking to Charlie had put a spring back in my step. Sharon wasn't as convinced as she wanted to know where her new car was! So I had to act fast. When I arrived to see Terry, it turned out to be at an old folks' sheltered accommodation and I was thinking to myself, Charlie, what the fuck have you sold me here!?

Terry was in his mid-seventies but his blue eyes sparkled like a young man's: "Would you like some Earl Grey and digestives?" I didn't hold back, not with the digestives, but in telling him all of my problems, giving him every single detail. It felt great to get it all off my chest. He sat quietly and listened. When I'd finally ran out of things to say I sat back waiting to hear his wisdom!

I can't exactly remember that much but the whole session was over in an hour so I gave him thirty notes and left feeling like a new man. What I do recall though was Terry urging me to get back on the racecourse as there was nothing to be frightened of: "It's what you're good at."

***

The very next day I took his advice and headed to Worcester which caused quite a stir with the other bookies when I set up my pitch: "Bloody hell, Gary, we thought you were brown bread" one joked. "We even had a whip round for a wreath, can we have our tenner back?"

This kind of thing happened everywhere I went for the next few weeks with people genuinely happy to see me, shaking my hand and slapping me on the back. I didn't have to force any smiles meeting back up with these people. Salt of the earth.

And it was as if I had never been away when in the first race my first punter asked for £400 to win £700 on the jolly. I only had £720 in my pocket after paying the £80 badge money but still took the bet. I couldn't cut the geezer back as I was Gary Wiltshire and had a reputation to uphold. Heading to the last flight and the 7/4 favourite was neck and neck with a 10/1 shot and together they went at it hammer and tongs up the run-in before the outsider went on to win by half a length.

As for the rest of the day, it was nip and tuck but we made a few more quid clearing £900 in total after all exes. The earnings were just the cherry on the top though as the main thing was that I had renewed energy and enthusiasm. Leaving the course that day I said to myself: "I'm back!"

1
Nice One Sirrell

Outside of Dettori Day and then being dubbed 'The Belly From The Telly' after my stint on the Beeb by *The Daily Mirror*, I am probably best known as the guy who won £500,000 having backed Norton's Coin at 200/1 to win the Cheltenham Gold Cup so we'll kick off with that.

That was back in 1990 so in today's terms that figure equates to about £1.2 million. This tale has been told before but only half of it. So now it's time to come clean on the full story explaining what happened when I turned up four days later to collect my biggest-ever pick up.

Actually, I should point out that it was half a mill divvied up 50-50 between myself and Johnny Earl, or JE as I used to call him, who I was working in partnership with and was the sharpest gentleman that I ever had the pleasure of dealing with. He had a distinctive look as didn't have a single hair on his body and always wore a trilby with a white mac when manning his pitch.

It was he who set me up as a bookie at Milton Keynes dogs going halves on his pitch. I eventually bought him out for £69,000 for his half share. That was his only pitch as that's how good he was. He was a mystery as nobody really knew his background including me as he wouldn't give much away but the man had serious connections.

FIFTY YEARS IN THE BETTING JUNGLE

So why did we fancy this supposed no-hoper trained by Sirrell Griffiths for the most prestigious jumps race of them all? This unheard-of dairy farmer with just three horses from Carmarthenshire with a permit licence so he was only allowed to train his own horses and later admitted that he only ran Norton's Coin, who he described as "an ugly plain chesnut," in the Gold Cup as the original plan was for another race but they missed the entry. I'm thinking the old Cathcart for which he would have been qualified and given his two-and-a-half miles form at the course.

The answer? *The Form Book*, readers, *The Form Book*. We knew how to read it and felt that he was more like a 33/1 chance rather than triple-figure odds so we took the best of the morning prices which was 200/1. His SP was 100/1 but he still returned the biggest-priced winner in the history of the race first run as a steeplechase in 1924. It was actually a flat race that first took place in 1819. Fountain of knowledge, me. Or is it just *Wikipedia*?

Although he finished last of six in the King George earlier that season, he was 33/1 that day to beat Desert Orchid in Dessie's own backyard of Kempton but was now as big as 200/1 to beat him in the Gold Cup on a course that the odds-on-favourite didn't like as he much preferred to race the other way round whereas Norton's Coin was proven at Cheltenham. He had blundered his chance away with mistakes on the first circuit at Kempton which you just can't do around that gaff so we were happy to throw that run out.

The form that we really liked was from the previous season when he won the big chase at Cheltenham's April Meeting which is called the Silver Trophy these days beating good horses like Beau Ranger,

Nice One Sirrell

Panto Prince and Golden Freeze and in doing so he also proved that he acted very well on the course. He also went on to win that same race two years later beating Waterloo Boy and Pegwell Bay. Ah, don't you like to reminisce?

On his final run before the Gold Cup, Norton's Coin had run a fair third off top weight over two-and-a-half miles at Newbury but he was totally unexposed over three miles and more so there was potential for lots of improvement.

Desert Orchid was to go off the odds-on jolly trying to win the race in back-to-back years but it was 15/2 bar him and just 12 runners, and one of those, unlike Norton's Coin, was a genuine 200/1 poke, so the Gold Cup had a real good each-way betting shape look about it. Plus, Dessie was also the oldest horse in the race aged eleven so no gimme to run up to last year's form.

Not only that but the second-favourite was a proper plodder being the dual Welsh Grand National winner on soft ground Bonanza Boy for Pipey and Scu, but the going description for the Gold Cup, believe it or not, was good-to-firm! Can you imagine that now!? It would be like World War III. So, there were obvious ground concerns for him and also for the previous year's second as Yahoo was another mudlark and had lost his form. And then there was Cavvies Clown. Runner-up two years earlier but he wasn't getting any younger and had started to become a right dodgepot and refused in the previous year's Gold Cup so David Elsworth was down at the start flapping his arms about just to help make him start.

Therefore, we decided that a proper bet should be stuck on Norton's Coin, especially as he was 200/1 in the morning with Con Wilson

FIFTY YEARS IN THE BETTING JUNGLE

Bookmakers in Northampton who also owned Wilcon Construction, and we staked £2,000 each-way. Admittedly, it was more for the place return of 50/1. Con was the brother of Lynn Wilson who was a prominent racehorse owner and the chairman of Northants Cricket Club.

Cavvies Clown did get away. Eventually. But he was already twenty lengths down jumping the first. Lovely. Nice to get one out of the way straight away. No way he was getting back that lost distance on fast ground.

After the first circuit, a group of seven had pulled about eight lengths clear of the remainder including Bonanza Boy who was being taken off his feet. He did eventually hook himself onto the back of the pack at one stage but it was short lived and he trailed in last of the eight finishers. So come half-way and I was already thinking just three more to beat for the 50/1 place payout.

Then at the third of the four ditches, a weakening Kildimo fell followed by Yahoo being hard ridden a fence later. Beautiful. And then Pegwell Bay started to feel the pinch shortly afterwards. Fantastic! All the while Graham McCourt was sitting towards the back of the leading pack on Norton's Coin intent on just watching on as the beaten horses dropped away one by one. Jumping the fourth-last and it looked like they now only had one rival to beat to hit the frame so I was getting extremely hopeful of collecting £98K's worth of profit for two large at 200s each-way at quarter the odds a pleasure.

Dessie under Richard Dunwoody had set out to make all the running but they were overtaken at the sixth-last fence by Ten Of Spades for Fulke Walwyn and Kevin Mooney who kept his lead until

Nice One Sirrell

rounding the home bend. Ten Of Spades had dropped back to fourth when he departed two out when he was beaten at which point we knew the 50/1 a place was in the bag barring a last-fence disaster. What a touch!

But hold on a minute what was this? Cavvies Clown had somehow been smuggled into the race from nowhere by Graham Bradley and was now on the verge of challenging! Thankfully those efforts to get back into the race eventually took their toll and he finished fourth beaten just a dozen lengths. Did losing all that ground at the start cost him the Gold Cup? Fuck knows but what did I care!

Before then and turning for home, Toby Tobias under Mark Pitman riding for his mother had been gifted a dream run up the inner which opened up like the Red Sea when Ten Of Spades drifted out, so that was their cue to make their bid for glory and the collective 'we' (because I know that you are with me on this) moved into second place. He couldn't, could he?

Meanwhile, Dessie being Dessie, began to rally and had gutsed his way back ahead of the collective 'us' with a mighty leap two out, so we were then demoted back into third. In the end though, his eleven-year-old legs finally gave way and he was beaten just under five lengths going down on his sword like the true warrior of the turf that he was.

Heading to the final fence and it was now a straight fight between Toby Tobias who took it with an advantage of a length over Norton's Coin. On the run-in though, our boy wore him down to score by three-quarters-of-a-length under a strong McCourt drive who looked much more the part than his opposing jockey when the chips were down.

They had only gone and done it causing one of the biggest racing shocks of all time and I had never felt an experience like it before in all my life. All Norton's Coin's official in-running comment in *The Form Book* read was: 'Always going well, led flat, all out.' That is exactly as straightforward a ride as it was. No fluke whatsoever.

Sirrell had only gone and done it too which led to a joyous chorus of *Nice One Cyril* ringing around the hotel bar where I was forced to watch the race from. By the way, did you know that the song was named after Cyril Knowles who played left back for Tottenham released before the 1973 League Cup Final against Norwich who they beat 1-0 that somehow reached No.14 in the charts? The spelling wasn't the same but even being a life-long Gooner I couldn't resist bursting out with a few bars. The lyrics 'Nice one Cyril, nice one son, nice one Cyril, let's have another one' really couldn't have been more apt. A literary classic I'm sure that you will all agree. Actually, the Ivor Novello Awards did as it won a prize off them for Best Novel or Unusual Song!

So why was I watching the Gold Cup from a hotel you might ask? We actually had tickets to attend Gold Cup Day but were forced to watch it from the Gloucester Hotel and Country Club as the manager had locked us in for not paying the bill. We had bought a Cheltenham Package from an agent in London but for whatever reason it hadn't been settled so he blocked off the route out of the car park to us and therefore all the other guests staying there.

Nice One Sirrell

When it finally got sorted by mid-afternoon there was not enough time to drive to the course to catch the Gold Cup so we headed down to the bar. None of the party of about a dozen, which included the legendary greyhound bookmaker John Power (John Jenkins) also called The Viking, knew that I had a big bet on Norton's Coin, they thought it was just a few quid so I certainly couldn't tell them how much I had won afterwards. At an SP of 100/1 though, it was obvious that I had still drawn a good earner so they joined me in the celebrations.

***

I always had an 11am meeting with Johnny on Mondays at his house to collect my wages behind Collingtree Golf Course, once the host of the British Masters, and the Monday after the Gold Cup before heading into Northampton to collect our half a million was no different. On this occasion though, JE had a surprise for me. A bottle of Johnny Walker. Not to drink so it turned out as I quickly discovered when he poured the contents all over my jumper that I was wearing as he wanted me to reek of alcohol when I turned up for the money.

I was greeted by the shop manager in the St James area, Jimmy's End, near where the Saints play. On arrival Alan told me that Con wanted me upstairs. Once I entered the top room, staring at me on the table was a black briefcase with the lid open with half a million pounds in cash, just like you see in scenes in the movies. Not being something that you see every day I was starry-eyed just looking at it.

His first words were: "You've been drinking" to which I replied: "No I ain't." I took another glance at the suitcase and then the words blurted out: "I don't want it. Stick it all on the favourite in the first at Folkestone" which was a 1/5 ON favourite for a novices' hurdle.

Con kept saying: "But you've been drinking, Gary" over and over so he was trying to do me a favour but I was insistent. This went on for a couple of minutes and the race was only ten minutes away but, seeing that I was adamant, he finally gave way and told me: "You've got a bet" and shut the case. I thanked him and walked straight out of his shop. It proved to be a performance worthy of winning an Oscar.

Now. The more curious amongst you might be thinking what the heck was I playing at? Had I taken total leave of all my senses? To be truthful, I didn't know absolutely everything myself as it wasn't my idea but, as JE was by far the cleverest man by a long way that I knew then or since who had his fingers in lots of pies, obviously he knew something that I didn't and told me that the horse should be 1/20 and not 1/5, so I went along with it. Bear in mind this was 35 years ago and if you read *The Barry Brogan Story* from his riding tales in the early 1970s then you will never have another bet in your life.

I was under instructions from JE that after leaving Con's office I was to call him from the nearest phone box to confirm that all £500,000 was on. There was now only five minutes to the off and a woman was on the phone. I had to wait but thankfully she finished in time. Upon hearing my confirmation, "Good" he replied, "We'll have another £100,000 in another five minutes. The only way this can get beat is if Lee Harvey Oswald makes a comeback."

On the way from leaving JE's house to Con's offices, he also wanted me to bring back a long twist and four Danish pastries from *Oliver*

Nice One Sirrell

Adams bakers. This I successfully managed to do without eating them. It also helped kill some time before seeing Con as we had timed it to arrive not long before the first race at Folkestone. JE seemed more concerned about me getting his pastries order right than the half a million we were about to bet, which he regarded as a racing certainty.

I didn't even watch the race as JE told me don't stay in the shop. So, by the time I had driven back to his house I didn't know the result. Upon opening the door to me, when I saw his face drop I thought oh no!: "What happened, did it fall?" I asked, to which he calmly replied words to the effect that it had pissed up, he had just noticed that I hadn't got the Danish pastries with me because I had left them in the car!

With our winnings we both bought properties opposite Panina Golf on the Algarve. We were having a drink at the local restaurant out there with our partners one night and I said something along the lines of how lovely this is being all here together to which he replied: "Don't worry Gal, when we stop doing business that will be the end." And he was true to his word as when our association came to an end, he didn't have any more use for me and I have not heard from him since. The last I knew he had moved to Florida decades ago. The man was a punting genius but a total enigma.

2
Learning My Trade

I was the school bookie. Like quite a few readers of this book, I'm sure? It was not so such much the betting jungle back then, more like the betting playground. I suppose that's where I first started to learn what was to become my trade. As it transpired, I learned it the hard way.

I should mention where it all began. As a teenage boy I loved watching *The Belle's Of St. Trinians*, obviously! My memory is a little bit hazy but for younger readers this was a comedy film from the 1950s set in an all-girls' boarding school focussing on the sixth-formers in their risqué school uniforms, some of which had criminal relations. The plot centred around them trying to save the school from bankruptcy by betting on the favourite for the Derby owned by a Sultan whose daughter was in residence but not before abducting the horse first. How it didn't win an academy award with a plot like that, I don't know!?

George Cole was most famous for playing Arthur Daley in *Minder* but before then his best-known role was the spiv Flash Harry who took the bets from the girls who had been raiding their parents' coffers. The brilliant Alastair Sim played both the headmistress and her twin brother Clarence the bookie and the cast also included Beryl Reid,

FIFTY YEARS IN THE BETTING JUNGLE

Joan Sims, Irene Handl and Sid James amongst other well-known actors of the day. I suppose you could say it was a forerunner to the 'Carry On' films which started a couple of years later. Needless to say, the horse won and the school was saved and after watching it I wanted to be the school bookie.

Just a tad slightly darker than St Trinian's, the scenes in the packed betting rings from *Brighton Rock* starring Richard Attenborough as Pinkie Brown in Graham Greene's classic about the bookmaker protection racket, also made an impact on a teenage Gary Wiltshire. I've still got a pitch in Lower Tatts at Brighton. It's value-less but I've kept it through my love of Brighton and the movie. The size of the crowds in the film were enormous and back in the day free buses were laid on for those travelling in from Victoria. I stayed at Butlins Holiday Hotel in nearby Saltdean. It's all flats now.

The modern-day TV equivalent of *Brighton Rock* is *Peaky Blinders* for which my boy Charlie auditioned for one of the leading characters and got through to last four in Edgbaston Park. Although he didn't get the part, he went on to appear on the West End stages and had his own cabaret show at John Fowler Holiday Parks where he was known as Charlie Wiltshire, The Brummie Crooner. What is it about gangsters and the betting ring that go hand in hand? Money, of course!

I've wheeled out in a few interviews that I left school with only two O-Levels; finding fish and chip shops and betting shops. Good for a one-line gag. Well, that's not quite accurate as I was a bright kid when it came to maths so learning odds came as easy to me as tying up a pair of shoelaces. I was always good with figures. Usually 36-24-36.

Learning My Trade

Given the weight that I ballooned to in adulthood, you will probably be surprised to learn that I was also very good at P.E. (physical education). So good that I even had trials as a goalkeeper for Leyton Orient. I don't know what it is about goalies and the Wiltshire's as my dad played between the sticks for Brentford and Charlie could have signed for Newcastle and Everton as a goalkeeper but decided that he wanted up play up front for the glamour instead thinking he was better at that. He wasn't. And now my grandson plays for his Under Sevens Sunday team as, would you believe it, a goalkeeper.

***

I was the school bookie at Highbury Grove, an all-boys comp in Islington. Sir Rhodes Boyson, who later went on to be in Maggie Thatcher's cabinet, he of the ridiculous mutton chops, baggy eyes and very strong Lancastrian accent, was the headmaster and he caned me for frequenting betting shops. Six of the best in front of the whole school.

I may have had the gift of the gab but there was no way that I could talk myself out of this one as he caught me red handed coming out of Hector MacDonald's on Highbury Corner roundabout one lunchtime. I just hated school dinners so used to head out for a bag of chips or an ice cream with the money that my mum gave me each day. Sometimes I skipped lunch just to have a bet with it but on one occasion Sir Rhodes just happened to be passing as I was walking out of the betting shop so I was bang to rights.

That afternoon he called me into his office and demanded the betting slip. As I knew it was a winning bet for about six quid I refused, telling him it was a winner. If I had effectively handed the winnings over to him then who knows, I may have been spared six cracks of the rod the next morning at assembly but for the winnings it was well worth it. I had this little trick so it didn't hurt too much by bending my fingers slightly rather than holding my palm out straight.

When Boyson was elected to the Houses of Parliament representing Brent North for the Tories in 1974 having earlier been a Labour councillor, he went on to be an outspoken supporter for the retention of corporal punishment in schools. You are not fucking kidding me! The man was a maniac for it. Rarely did an assembly pass without a boy feeling the warmth of his cane. Much later in life I did meet him again when I was working for the BBC up at Aintree: "Hello sir, remember me, you caned me for gambling?" He was a very old man then so was probably being polite when he said that he did. He caned so many of us I can't believe that he recalled me for a minute. My daughter Kelly became a head mistress and would find these tales abhorrent.

In June 1970, I took plenty of schoolyard bets for the Derby favourite Nijinsky by which time I had moved to Bishop Stopford School in Enfield. So, after Lester Piggott had guided him to victory for Vincent O'Brien, I had to skive the next week off school wheelin' and dealin' to pay off my debts. I was aged sixteen at the time so didn't really know exactly why I was laying him to lose so much money except for the fact that the bookies always win don't they? Trust me to pick the only horse to win the Triple Crown in the last 90 years!

Cartahatch Lane was a big council estate where I used to go knocking door to door selling fruit. My parents had a flower stall in Leather Lane between 12-2pm in Holborn where amongst their

Learning My Trade

regular customers back in the early sixties when I was only a little kid sat on the corner of the stall was Violet Kray, mother of the notorious East End gangsters who sometimes were with her and used to give me two bob and say get yourself a bar of chocolate.

The fruit stall opposite was run by Freddie Carr who used to give some of what was left over at 2pm to my dad at a fraction of the asking price which I would then mark up and sell at three times the price round the houses that same afternoon. Peaches, mainly, but also strawberries or whatever was in season. I used to string a box around my neck and head to the most densely-populated areas.

We were pally with the Everest family from that estate and Lou especially. He used to love a bet and taught me about the art of gambling. He was in charge of the Enfield Working Men's Club so a real face in the community who I looked up to. Everyone knew him. Throughout my life I have always preferred listening to and dealing with people much older than me to learn from them.

Lou often used to slide me into the Top House pub where Chas & Dave performed on Sunday mornings as did the comedian Jimmy Jones who was proper old school. I loved Chas & Dave all the way up until when Chas Hodges died. *Gertcha*, *London Girls*, *Margate*, *Rabbit*, *Sideboard Song*, *Snooker Loopy* and of course the classic, *Musn't Grumble*. Being a Gooner I had to draw the line at *Glory, Glory Tottenham Hotspur* though with Ossie Ardiles. I went on to be mates with the drummer, Micky Burt. Give it some stick Mick was what Chas always told him mid-song for his drum solo. Great times.

Lou later went on to become my tic-tac man at Rochester greyhound stadium where a famous big coup was landed in 1978 which John

FIFTY YEARS IN THE BETTING JUNGLE

McCririck covered for *The Sporting Life*. It ended up with a long, legal battle that lasted, get this, for seven years. I know what you're thinking but don't worry I wasn't involved!

Two dogs trained by Jack Purvis won both the sprint heats (277 metres) of a dual-distance competition (the other being over 901 metres) at 33/1 and 4/1 which had been backed off course in the London shops winning a reputed £350,000 or over £2.5 million today. This was dog racing so an incredible figure. Come the second race over the marathon trip though, one of the dogs was then withdrawn and the other finished last, not staying the distance.

The two dogs were brought over from Ireland and were pure sprinters so had no chance in the longer race so the coup planners just doubled them up for the sprint heats. The rumour was that no one was backing them on track despite the four standing bookies knocking their odds out because there was four dubiously-connected big heavies standing in front of each of their pitches stopping punters from doing so. If anyone wanted to back any of those two dogs then they would have been knocked out quicker than the prices on the board so the SP in the shops could be as big as possible.

BOLA, the big bookies' trade body, advised its members not to pay out even though the greyhound authorities found no rule breaking had taken part. The police submitted a report to the Director of Public Prosecutions who decided to take no action. This then resulted with eight hundred betting shops having had their locks superglued from the outside so staff couldn't enter the premises to get into work. Despite all this, eventually the Judge reached a verdict that the bookies didn't have to pay a single penny.

Learning My Trade

I've still got twelve tubes of the Loctite Superglue in the shed. Only kidding!

We only lasted a few meetings at Rochester as there were far too many sharp characters which meant that it just wasn't profitable. Curly Wilson was the top bookie at that track and the only way you beat him was with a sledgehammer and then you weren't a cert. The track closed down in 1979.

Before then and straight from school I became a board marker in the Ladbrokes head office in Ganton Street in the West End of London. I was seventeen so too young to work in the shops. I used to wet the coloured chalks so it stood out more than the other young board markers but I didn't take to it, not only because of the travelling but being stuck inside all day just wasn't me. I needed to be out and about ducking and diving.

A couple of years earlier still I was a part-time kennel hand at Northaw near Potter's Bar where Camira Flash was trained by Randy Singelton for none other than the Duke of Edinburgh, Prince Philip, when he won the Greyhound Derby at White City. I must have missed that episode of *The Crown*! He actually only finished fourth in his semi-final but another dog was disqualified for fighting so he was promoted to third. Although then into the final, he was sent off as the rank outsider at 100/8 but from trap four he beat the second-least fancied dog into second when winning by a length after the 4/6 favourite Shady Parachute missed the break.

How times have changed. There were sixteen dog tracks in Greater London back then but sadly now only Romford remains.

***

FIFTY YEARS IN THE BETTING JUNGLE

A ruse which I dreamt up to fund my teenage betting came when I was living in Enfield. Knowing that mum and dad were working at the market, I invited school mates back to the house for bacon sandwiches and sold them at 10p. If I could get six mates round then that would pay for my 5p Yankee which came to 55p at Brookes of Enfield Wash next to the half-way house pub opposite the school. Very handy. Being far too young to walk in, I waited outside looking for people to put the bets on for me. After a while I got to know the regulars who then didn't need asking. Let's call it entrepreneurial spirit.

This money-making exercise was all going very well until one day my parents shut up early and came home at lunchtime to find six lads effectively raiding their fridge. I had a healthy appetite so until that day my mum thought that I had just been feeding myself. But rather than getting the hump with me she took the opposite view and thought what a lovely, thoughtful boy I was doing this for his friends. So she started buying extra bacon going forward. This meant that I could increase my stakes to a 10p Yankee. To her dying day she never knew what I was up to, God love her.

I knew not to try it on Mondays though as that was the day off for market stall holders, costermongers and publicans, many of which then got on the train for a day at the races. Always by train. I wonder if Windsor having so many Monday evening meetings stems back from that?

I don't know if I was madder on racing or gambling? Probably gambling but like many kids who loved racing I invented my own horseracing game which kept me occupied and out of trouble for

Learning My Trade

hours on end. It consisted of the four kings in a pack of cards laid out in a line. As for the other forty-eight cards, I would turn them over one after one and if a club came out then the King of Clubs moved up one length and so on. They were generally eight-furlong races so whoever got to eight first won the race. I called it The King's Heath. I don't know why. Later in life I discovered there was a dog track in Kings Heath in Birmingham that ran five-dog races on Saturday afternoons.

At around the same time I was the bookie for numerous Donkey Derby's at Coombe Haven Caravan Park in St Leonards-on-Sea. My parents owned Number 42 Meadowbank and every week the camp used to a organise a series of races. So when we were having a break there, rather than making a book on it, instead I ran a mini-tote and made myself a commission of £40 or £50 profit. Not bad if I say so myself as a fifteen-year-old flogging tickets for 10p a pop. Certainly less stressful to be guaranteed a nice draw than making a book.

***

Now some of you might have wondered why I never tried to make it in the world of pro punting?

Actually, I did once in my very early-twenties but what did I know back then? Most of us think that we're better at gambling than we actually are and suffice to say it didn't last long. I don't want to get too autobiographical in a book of disclosing betting jungle stories but there are a couple of tales directly relating to that period of my life why I felt forced to try punting professionally that I can honestly say looking back now, I am truly ashamed of.

FIFTY YEARS IN THE BETTING JUNGLE

I was all set to be married to a Jewish girl from Walthamstow called Susan Gosling. She was from a well-to-do background and owned a beautiful, white E-Type jag with lovely red seats that only managed about fourteen miles to the gallon which she let me use but I couldn't afford to fill it up very often. What she saw in me, heaven only knows?

The wedding was all set, the synagogue booked in Southgate, the King David Suite for Jewish weddings paid for by her parents, the suits had already been hired from Moss Brothers and the invites all sent out. Eleven days before the big day, I had to meet the rabbi to organise the plans and then he hit with me with it. I needed to be booked in to be circumcised beforehand!

I didn't know if this was common practice or not but Susan, who was a good ten years older than me, had not said a word. I had been on the receiving end of a few gambles in my time and, truth be told, as the day got nearer and nearer, I didn't particularly fancy this one.

I was booked in for the Tuesday before the Saturday wedding. On the Monday before the operation, I went to Fontwell Park in her Jag with £400 in my pocket where I happened to have a very good day turning it into over £2,000 but my head was still spinning thinking about the following morning being scared of putting Little Gary under the knife. So being a coward and now also flush with readies, instead I drove to Weymouth and boarded the overnight ferry to Jersey.

Then I got my old mate Wilf to arrive outside the ferry terminal and drive the car back to Susan in Blackhorse Road in Walthamstow having left the key on the top of the back tyre with a letter left inside saying that I just couldn't go through with it. I couldn't even tell her on the phone, let alone face to face. What a bastard I was. It wasn't

Learning My Trade

quite leaving her at the altar but not far off it. I was in tears writing it as knew I was badly letting her and everyone else down.

It was over forty years later when curiosity got the better of me. We had not spoken or seen each other since the day I took her Jag to Fontwell. I don't how I did it but somehow plucked up the courage to get back in touch with Susan with a bit of help and she got a big shock when picking up the phone. We agreed to meet up at Theydon Bois tube station near Loughton and when I saw her waiting for me, I started to well up. We went to a Miller & Carter Steakhouse where she couldn't have been any nicer, which made me feel even worse for what I had done but said that it was all for the best as she was very happily married with beautiful children and grandchildren. And that was it and we parted company on good terms.

***

Once in Jersey, after I had stood up both the surgeon and Susan (but thankfully saved my foreskin), I thought to myself, what the hell am I going to do now?

The one thing that I did know was that there was no tax deducted from betting shops in Jersey unlike in the UK where it was 9% so I thought I'd try and have a go at making a living punting. On the ferry over I met a bloke who was renting a six-bedroom house in St Helier so I took one of the rooms for £50 a week. After laying down a deposit of £250 this was going to be the new life for me and I couldn't tell a single soul after what I had done.

In Red Houses about five miles away there was a Ladbrokes plus an independent called E Coombes of Greenwich so after a bus ride I spent most of my afternoons floating between the two. I was holding my own until the inevitable big blowout came which knocked out my float and so after just seven weeks that ended my only attempt at being a pro punter.

At around the time when I blew my betting bank, I met a guy called Maurice in the Laddys who was dressed immaculately. He was barred from Coombes but wanted a monkey on a 2/1 favourite with them as they were going the bigger price so he asked me if I would place the bet for him. The horse won and I returned handing him back £1,500. There and then he said: "Now I know I can trust you" and he changed my life for the next six months.

Later that same afternoon in his Merc he took me back to St Helier and bought me a lovely evening suit and said: "Gary, you're working for me now." Turns out that he owned the Hawaiian Nightclub in Portelet Bay and my job was to introduce the compere for the evening cabaret plus the six Hawaiian dancing girls. What a job, though I had to sing and I didn't exactly croon like Frank Sinatra but still had to pull off *Fly Me To The Moon*.

This meant that I could also give up the room that I was renting for a bungalow by the sea which Maurice owned on the site of the nightclub with Butlins Holiday Camp nearby. After the show I used to head there most nights. At that time, I weighed in at only around 12st and had a cheeky personality with an element of charm so, living with six supermodels, what days they were! Ellen from Wallasey was my favourite.

Maurice looked after me like a father plus on top I used to get around £300 a week in tips from the customers I looked after. I had

Learning My Trade

to move out at the end of the season but what a six months' that was and then head back home to face a very different kind of music.

When I did my runner five days before the wedding, no one knew where I was or what I was doing. Not event my parents. To everyone I knew apart from Wilf, I had just vanished off the face of the earth. So when I returned to Enfield in late October and knocked on 900 Great Cambridge Road, my mum opened the door in floods of tears and told me that she thought I was dead. To think that I put her through that still pains me now. My dad was also in tears which I had never seen before. For all they knew I was on the missing list. I was one inconsiderate, selfish fucker.

I still visit St Brelade's Bay for an occasional break and stay at L'Horizon Beach Hotel where Camacho, who was a waiter in the restaurant and remembers me from the old days, is still working there some fifty years later.

3
In A Right Old Flap

For those of you unaware of what flapping tracks are given that they barely exist anymore, they are independently-run greyhound tracks.

Contrary to what a lot of people think there is absolutely nothing illegal about them. They were all legit, just unaffiliated to the governing body, the Greyhound Board of Great Britain. The tracks were safe and welfare was paramount so anyone could turn up anywhere with any dog, usually those that had been retired or were just too slow to make the grade, and then race them against each other, sometimes even walking them to the track from their house.

In order to set up my first pitch at a flapping track at the age of twenty, I had to get a bookmaker licence from Stony Stratford Magistrates Court. In awarding it to me, they saved me from a life of I don't know what because, and there's no other way to put it, I was a chronic, compulsive, mug punter. Up until I was granted my licence, I was blowing my day's earnings in the shops around Dunstable on the way back home with the exception of £50 that I wouldn't touch as handed that over to my first wife Phyllis for housekeeping. I only learned how to become a good punter when I became a bookie by watching the mistakes of others.

FIFTY YEARS IN THE BETTING JUNGLE

I was almost turned down as when the Judge asked the court if there were any police objections, a copper stood up and announced that I had been drunk and disorderly in Bridlington. But I have never been to Bridlington in my life before or afterwards. Where is it? At this point my solicitor instructed me to stay seated and keep schtum whilst the Judge looked me up and down, smiled, and said anyone of your age is entitled to go over the top once or twice before wishing me good luck and sending us on our way.

***

I started off at Nutts Lane flapping track in Hinckley, Leicestershire, where all sorts of shenanigans were occurring on Wednesday and Saturday nights. I made it my business to get close to a local called Joey 'The Watch' Cope who was a trainer but also the best judge of a dog at that track. Over an educational few weeks, he gave me the lowdown to the extent that I was confident enough of winning a few bob off the local, hardened punters.

I used to sell him replica watches that I brought up from the market in Hatton Garden and he doubled his money by selling them at the flapping track, hence how he got his name. I didn't want anyone else to know that they originally came from me so, I used to help him out with dodgy watches to flog, and he used to help me out with info. So, there was gold to be found in them thar hills as Mark Twain said but not before borrowing the family allowance to fund the book from Phyllis who was an angel.

On the pitch next to me stood the Northamptonshire bookie Lesley Wootton who was the spit of Greengrass from *Heartbeat* played by Bill Maynard. Bill lived locally and was a punter at Hinckley and

In A Right Old Flap

based his character on Wootton. I couldn't make up my mind about Lesley, though. At times he was a saviour lending me a few quid if I had taken some early knocks but he could also be a nasty piece of work as he then let everyone there know about it. And he had a thunderous voice so everyone could hear him indiscreetly blurting: "You cockneys have got plenty of mouth but you ain't got money." He was much older than me and I just had to take it and suffer in silence as I was dependent on him at times.

Eventually it got to the point when enough was enough so I hatched a plan to get my own back. The town of Hinckley was best known for being the home of the hosiery business so, alongside my sidekick Gary Selby, we decided that we were going to properly pull his pants down. It took a couple of months to set up the sting but boy was it worth it.

After having a good run at the track, I no longer had the need to borrow any cash so with some of the earnings I bought a decent greyhound called Exclusive Native for £400 which was plenty for a dog back then. We didn't want any old dog for what we had planned as we only had one shot at it. I stuck him in training with The Watch.

Exclusive Native was previously trained by John Peterson and ran regularly at Oxford. Once we had bought him, we ran him three times at Hinckley under the name of Black Trevor where he finished stone last each time following a large bowl of sausages. That put us in prime position to then enter him for a mediocre handicap getting a head start. As far as flapping was concerned back then, anything goes.

Once we found out the handicapper had given him trap two with a six yards' start over the scratch dog over 315 metres, there would be no trip to the butchers that week for Trev. Plus, as luck would have it, The Watch also trained the one dog who had a two metres' start over us but he hadn't had three large sausages that day, more like thirty-three so we knew that we had nothing in front of us.

What we needed to find now was a stooge to put the bet on with Wootton. As he was an ignorant misogynist, we decided that it should be a woman. So, we met up with a girl called Sharon who worked as a part-time barmaid at the Hinckley Island Hotel who agreed to play her role. We handed over £155 on our way to the track and told her to wait until our dog drifted out to 5/1.

She was knocking off work at 7pm and Black Trevor was all set to run for his life in the fourth race at 8.15pm but five minutes before the off there was no sign of Sharon and we started thinking the worst. Finally, there she was standing on the rails.

All the dogs on all the boards opened up at 2/1. Generous, weren't we? But that's the way it worked so not to get caught out on a live one at first show and then we would push the prices out, which happens in double-quick time.

I needed Black Trevor's price pushed out more quickly than most so in the space of the next two minutes I kept crossing the odds out and updating: 5/2, 3/1, 7/2, 4/1, 9/2. Still not a bean thankfully, so then the magic 5/1. Not wanting to get left behind, Wootton was keeping pace and then went 6s before me and in stepped Sharon. He couldn't hedge it with anyone as he went biggest. He then glanced sideways and gave a look to me as if to say, look how I've just stolen that bet off you.

In A Right Old Flap

At that point I left my pitch and headed to the other end of the line and got £80 on at 5s with Lloyd Coyle who was a betting shop manager for William Hill and a part-time bookie at the dogs and another £80 with Ron Cooper of Coventry whilst Gary had £50 on with Dave Smith of Loughborough. There was a school teacher at the other end called Hutchinson and Gary knew that he could get another ton on with him so did so. Unlike with Wootton, I felt a bit bad stitching those guys up but when you have an edge, you have an edge. Everything had gone like clockwork so now it was all up to Black Trevor.

Rounding the first bend and he had already picked up the one dog after his large lunch and then he was gone. Out of here. Nothing could get near him and he won by five lengths. We'd had it right off and I certainly wasn't going to miss Sharon picking her up £900 off Wootton. He wasn't best pleased and immediately smelled a rat barking at her to tell him who really backed it as "it clearly wasn't you!" At this point I thought she might crack but she remained tight-lipped as he effectively threw the money at her. Although the profit was very nice, £2180 in total, the main thing was that he hadn't taken it well which was the main point of why we did it.

Sharon sloped off out of the track and, as pre-planned, we two Gary's weighing in at 28st and 25st must have looked some sight sat in our mini cooper in the car park of Barnacles Fish Restaurant to meet her at 10pm. Well, 10.05pm came and went and still no sign of Sharon. We didn't know her very well so I'd be lying if I said that it didn't cross my mind that she might have done a runner.

FIFTY YEARS IN THE BETTING JUNGLE

Shortly afterwards a set of headlights flashed outside from a small car. I couldn't be seen with her after what we had just pulled off so Selby headed outside and took the cash from the car window, handing back a ton for her part, which she was over the moon with. That was a lot of money for a part-time waitress in those days but she had earned every single penny of it. "Mum's the word" he whispered and she understood exactly what that meant before disappearing off into the night.

After that episode I would sometimes catch Wootton eyeing me up in a strange way so wonder if he had an inkling who was behind it? If he did work it out then he never let on as that would have been too embarrassing for him to admit that I had royally tucked him up. In fact, it knocked some of the spite out of him and we became a lot friendlier as the years passed so I even started to feel some sense of guilt but remained schtum. I think he also respected me a lot more than in the early days when he realised that I had become a damn good bookie.

It was a sad day when Hinckley closed down in 2006 and even sadder when we lost Lesley Wootton in 2024. He was one of Northampton's finest and I attended his funeral. I have got a heart, I really have.

That wasn't the only tale involving Black Trevor but this time we never got paid out. It was at Coalville and we had backed him again. Not to win fortunes but we fancied him legitimately this time and he was four lengths clear at the final bend when Sharon started shouting out: "Oi Oi, call the copper, they won't catch this one." Straight away the red light appeared indicating a void race.

In A Right Old Flap

In all my years at Hinckley this was the only time I ever saw a red light appear. The rumour was that the boss of the track had backed his own dog in the same race who was getting beat so the instructions pre-race would be to void it on the spot if he looked in trouble so he could get his money back. You hear stories about hare operators looking out for secret signs from the stands in certain situations, or like floodlights going out on a low-level football match, and this was the closest I came to seeing it in the flesh. As for Trevor, once he retired, we made sure we gave him a good home.

One post-script to the Black Trevor tales. The putter-oner was Sharon Broadley who was a young amateur jockey at the time for David Wintle and later went on to ride some of my horses. Oh, and we also have been partners living together for the last twelve years!

***

Looking back, a funny story now that I didn't think was at all funny at the time was when I was betting at Warwick flapping track on this one hundred-yards' dash. As usual I opened up at 2/1 for all six dogs to feel out what was hot and what was not. You literally have no idea the true identity of these dogs.

Within seconds up walks this geezer from Birmingham who wants £200 on trap two. I said: "I'll lay you £100, mate" and knocked it down to Evens. A minute or so later he steps up again wanting £200 at Evens. Once again, I said he could have half the stake and cut the dog to 1/2 ON. Another minute or so and he's back for more and now wants £400 on to win two. I said he could have £200 and cut it again into 1/3 ON. And so it went on and I'm thinking, fucking hell, what's going on here? After then laying him at Carpet On to half

FIFTY YEARS IN THE BETTING JUNGLE

his requested stakes he told me: "You'll make a bloody good butcher, son, the way you keep cutting me." The last bet I took off him was at 1/4 ON. He wanted four hundred to win one, so I gave him that one.

Coming out on the traps, and on my kids' life, the two dog stumbles and falls, in a one-hundred yards' dash. So naturally I'm thinking we've had a right touch here! A few seconds later he's not only got up off the deck but he's pissed in by three lengths.

So, up comes the punter for his winnings a couple of minutes later looking very pleased with himself and told me smiling in his strong Brummie accent: "Son, I bet you think you're clever, don't you? Let me tell you something. Those six dogs? I own all of them. Five are pets, one's fifteen, another's thirteen and only one of them can run." Turns out his name was Arthur Caine, a businessman who owned the Working Men's Club near Perry Barr. Apparently, he kept pulling off this trick up and down the country and I was his mark this time as he'd been tipped off that I took a bet.

If you are a big fan of greyhound racing and want to watch eight old boys who look and sound like they planned the Hatton Garden heist harking back to the good old days, the strokes pulled, the bent managers and how some of it was gangster-run at certain greyhound and flapping tracks way back in the day, then I recounted that tale and a few others in a seven-part series called *Flapping* on *YouTube* put together by Wapping Assassin TV in 2021. Charlie Kray ran Portsmouth and most of the flapping tracks were frequented by naughty people who couldn't get an official trainers' licence.

***

In A Right Old Flap

At Hinckley on Wednesdays, they used to have one race restricted for dogs that had never even trialled before. Therefore, we were even more in the dark about them than the other races. Nobody knew what they were up against including the bookies. For just this race there was an entry fee of £50 and the winning owner took the lot. So as usual I went 2s the field first show. Next to me I heard Ron Cooper take a big bet on the one dog at 2/1 so I immediately scrubbed off the bottle and went Evens. But the same punter then came up to me and had an even £400.

Then I could hear another punter having fortunes on the bottom dog at 2/1 so again I cut him into Evens after which I laid him an even monkey. Then in world record time straight afterwards I could hear a third set of owners wanting to lump the four dog who was supposed to be the champion sprinter of Scotland so, again, I cut it into Evens sharpish before they approached me and I availed them of an even £400. It's fair to say that this was the only time in my life when I had ever laid Evens three times in any event.

As it turned out all three got beat as Ginger McGee had a black dog who I knew all about in the same race who went and won, so overall I ended up winning over £2,000 in one race which at a flapping track was unheard of, especially in a no-trial race.

Ginger was originally called 'The King of the Flaps' before he went on to become a licenced trainer and then seven-times British Champion but on the sly he still occasionally liked to lay one out at a flapping track even though licenced trainers were not to be seen at the premises. Therefore, when he used to come up to Hinckley on a Wednesday night, he got someone to put on the bet, stayed in his car, waited for the dog to win, got paid, and drove the dog back to its kennels afterwards. A proper smash and grab job.

***

When we had a pitch at Clacton, for a while back in the eighties we had a nice little earner set up with the boss of the track John Old who loved a pound note. If there was a close finish for one meeting it would be called a head, another meeting a short-head, another a dead-heat and another a neck, mixing it up. There was no official photo finish mechanism, just the naked eye.

On one night two dogs went past the line together. Inseparable. So up I went with 1/2 a short-head, 3/1 a dead-heat, 3/1 a head and 10/1 a neck. This holidaymaker from the north staying at nearby Butlins was standing on the line so he had £100 on a short-head with a £25 saver on the dead-heat for effectively what he thought was a draw-no-bet cert.

Little did he know that night that it had already been preordained that all winning distances in tight finishes would be given out as a neck. If anyone had wanted to have a bet on a neck with me then I would have just moved them on saying don't be silly, save your money. Once the result was announced over the Tannoy and the winning distance was given as a Gregory, the punter had to be given oxygen to get him off the deck!

4
Oxford Dogs

After leaving school, funnily enough I didn't make it to Oxford University. I did, however, make it to Oxford dogs. It took me a while to work my way up as I started off as a clerk for Derek Burrows at Milton Keynes when I was aged twenty. He used to pull up in a jag in his lovely leather coat and I wanted a piece of that.

Haringay was the first track that I attended as it was a regular Friday night out for my mum and dad. I loved the atmosphere and it got me hooked on betting. They used to give me £3 for the night so I put on 10p combination forecasts with three dogs so 60p a race, therefore if I didn't draw in the first five races I was gone.

Back in those days bookies were always kitted out in smart suits and lovely shoes so I looked up to them. I've got a thing about shoes. I think that they are a good way of trying to quickly weigh someone up that you've never met before. Now it's jeans and trainers on a lot of them. Call me old-fashioned but I think that there should at least be some element of dress code for bookies like Tony May insists is the case at Ascot. I say to bookies today to take pride in your appearance, this is a place of work. How hard can it be?

***

FIFTY YEARS IN THE BETTING JUNGLE

After learning the ropes with Del Boy, as Derek was known in the game, not long after Hinckley flapping track had closed down and just as I was getting my feet under the table at a NGRC track at Leicester, that shut down too. Therefore, I got myself a pitch at Oxford which raced on Tuesday, Friday afternoons and Saturday.

Being the new kid on the block then, I was slipped in right at the end in Pitch No. 8 but my clientele grew steadily. The only reason I got in was because Mick Wheble also moved from Leicester when that track closed down and I bribed him with a load of Crombie double-breasted overcoats like what Tommy Shelby wears in *Peaky Blinders*. I picked then up in Leather Lane for next to nothing as they were all sized wrong.

I recall one Champion Hurdle Day in March in those early years, the prestigious Pall Mall Stakes taking place which even today is still Oxford's biggest race since it was transferred from Haringay in 1988, and Harry Redknapp won it in 2007 with Ballymac Charley for the training legend, Charlie Lister. A distinguished Grade 1 category race with a long history first run in 1935, it was considered a good stepping stone to the Greyhound Derby a few months later.

It wasn't being covered on Sky or being shown in the betting shops so the only way to watch the action unfold was to be at the track in Sandy Lane for a stonking night out and thousands used to heed the call for this particular race, plenty of which had stopped off from Cheltenham on the way back to London. Little old Gal was still perched right at the end of the line but business was booming to the extent that my turnover for that one night featuring eight races was £69,000.

Oxford Dogs

We only ended up in front by a few hundred but I'd give my right arm to experience the buzz of that night again. A remarkable turnover by any standards, let alone for a provincial track, so goodness knows how much Peter Day and Jack Cowan in the No. 1 and No. 2 pitches took.

***

I was going to take this story to my dying day but, apologies Mr Gary Baydon, it's time to come clean.

One way we survived at Oxford was coming up with the idea surrounding the one hurdle race on the card every Friday. There was always a good atmosphere on a Friday afternoon as plenty of workers from the Mini car plant behind the track in Cowley came along after finishing their shift.

Our scheme for this one race was that we would bung the groundsman a pony to bang the inside panel hard into the ground for the two hurdles down the back straight so they stood more upright. No one would be able to see this as no one was ever over that side of track. However, the inside dogs could spot this approaching the hurdle so they would then check up only fractionally to jump them so losing ground in the air whereas the outside dogs would fly through the hurdle as usual. A fraction is all you need most of the time at the speed dogs can clock.

We had to shake it up week by week though or everyone would be latching on to the high numbers so the following week we would ask the groundsman to hammer down the outside panel. We got away with it for two-to-three years betting the forecasts and tricasts in the shops in London but not on the track as we couldn't give anything away. The poor racing manager used to scratch his head wondering why low numbers were favoured one week and high the next week. Sorry again, Gary.

I must stress the dogs were never in danger of falling or hurting themselves as the hurdles were basically made of air and straw so dogs could run straight through them. They just had to make a very slightly wider arc so losing some momentum in the air.

It was Dave Rossi who put the bets on for us. He was a London cabbie who used to dress up as an American tourist and with a copy of *USA Today* underneath his arm whilst frequenting the West End betting shops to give the impression he was a mug. He used to place six £100 combination forecasts and six £50 tricasts. Eight or nine times out of ten we used to get the forecast up and two or three times we hit the jackpot of the tricast.

Dave used to get round the staff to not refuse the bets by way of a little sweetener. He told them that he was visiting his daughter at Uni but if they wanted any gold sovereigns which he showed them, then they could have them at £40 a pop when they were worth a minimum £60-70 which is what he bought them for at cost that morning in Hatton Garden. Therefore, they knew they could make an easy score or more for nothing. He'd say take the sovereigns now and I'll collect the money the next time I'm here which meant that when he came to pick up the winnings and they wanted a top up, that they would obviously let him place bets again. He was the best. So why did we stop a good thing? Here's why.

***

Oxford Dogs

My career was on the rise but an incident one Friday afternoon at Oxford halted my progress. All the races were being televised into the high-street betting shops when I was accused of trying to manipulate the odds.

One bookies' rep from a large organisation attempted to shorten up a dog that I had priced up at 4/1. He passed me a grand and I cut it to carpet, 3/1. A minute later, he then gave me another grand but this time I left the odds unchanged. "Shorten the dog up then" he told me so that the price in the shops would be cut to which I replied: "No, have some more on." He refused so the odds remained at 3/1.

My reasoning, and the rep didn't know this, was that I had already taken a big bet on another dog from a local, big punter Phil Matton so was merely trying to get a balanced book. As luck would have it, both dogs got beaten so I ended up winning a right good few grand and went home a happy man.

That was until I walked through the door as the phone was already ringing and it was John Blake, the general manager from the track: "Gary I've got to expel you from the Friday (BAGS) meetings but your position for the night meetings remains unaffected." BAGS stands for Bookmakers Afternoon Greyhound Service for the shops so those meetings are run by and for the benefit of the high-street firms.

Even though I knew the answer, I asked him why, but didn't get a reply which only confirmed my suspicions. This large high-street firm had thrown their toys out of the pram. The news spread through the industry like wildfire and I was even invited by *Channel 4 Racing* to appear on *The Morning Line* and be interviewed by Big Mac. Given it was a horseracing show, looking back, I don't quite know why but I went along with it.

John regularly referred to himself as a failed bookmaker and started with a dolly question: "Are you are gambler?" I went straight on the front foot and drove it firmly to the boundary: "John, you know all bookies are gamblers, some win, others lose, like yourself."

He didn't like that very much so for the next delivery he tossed in a not-so-well disguised googly: "Who was the bookmaker that was trying to push down the price of the dog?" Well, with Johnny Francome having warned me on the set beforehand that this question was coming so to be ready for it, I just stuck my front leg out and padded that one out of harm's way. I'm not a grass and never will be. I was never going to reveal who it was and I was not going to give McCririck his headline.

That same afternoon after driving to Market Rasen, I was on the rails and the same rep who had tried to shorten up the dog at Oxford approached my pitch. I thought to myself, hello, he's got some nerve but I bore him no malice. At the end of the day, he was trying to do his job and make a living just like me and it wasn't his decision to have me banned from BAGS meetings. He pointed to a 16/1 outsider: "A thousand at 2/1 please, Gary." That was his way of saying thank you for me keeping schtum. A life lesson, don't ever be a snitch, no good ever comes of it.

I had twelve great years at Oxford but reluctantly decided to give up my pitch there at the end of the century. Greyhound racing was suffering even back then and most of my big wins were on horseracing

Oxford Dogs

tracks. I was proud of what I had achieved there as started out in Pitch No.8 and ended up on numero uno but betting was on the change. Something called the exchanges were attracting interest.

I kept my hand in though by keeping my pitch at Milton Keynes which was closer to home so it was a sad day on Boxing Day 2005 when their stadium which was also used for speedway closed down. After it became derelict it suffered a major fire resulting in its demolition to be replaced by? You've guessed it. Another bleedin' housing estate.

When I had the pitch at Milton Keynes, without being funny, as I had been dealing with sharp characters all my life in London, when it came to a new town, I felt ahead of everyone else there. I had learned to live on my wits and instincts in the street markets so felt that I had an advantage.

Seven years later and even Oxford was gone too, so now all my old tracks had run their race. However, to my great surprise and delight, Oxford reopened in 2022 and now races on Monday, Friday and Saturday, with speedway on Wednesday, Thursday and Sunday. Come on lads and lasses, pull your finger out, you must be able to find something on Tuesdays! Seriously, though, a great effort to secure a ten-year lease by Kevin Boothby after a hard-fought campaign.

***

In the early part of this century, I bought a dog to give to my son Danny who has special needs. Danny was thirteen at the time and loved greyhound racing so we put him in training with Trevor Cobbold known as King of the Carrots as he used to grow and sell them.

FIFTY YEARS IN THE BETTING JUNGLE

He rang me up one day when he was poorly with cancer to tell me that the dog *will* win the A7 race at Mildenhall that night so make sure to bring Danny along. Although he was very ill, he made the effort to also be there. He had all the Decoy-named dogs and was a top trainer and top bloke with a top family. He sadly died only a few days later.

True to his word the dog won but he was short so we didn't back him - the main thing was that Danny was there to watch him win and then pick up the trophy on the stage and take it home with him. What a night and what a memory.

***

After all the TV work dried up, out of the blue last summer I was approached by Mike Davis to appear on a new greyhound show he was putting together on *YouTube* called *Gone To The Dogs Live*. A real enthusiast and big owner in the sport, I suppose you could say that he is the J P McManus of greyhound racing.

Mike joined forces with the fourteen-times champion trainer Mark Wallis in 2023 to be his private trainer and has given a breath of new life to the sport. I used to work with his parents at Northaw when I was a teenager but, regardless, I was keen to be part of this new concept so was delighted to accept and be back on the TV cameras again and have been an ever-present since. This means I can still enjoy my nights at the dogs at the big tracks eight-to-ten times a year.

5
Getting To The Point

Point-to-pointing is where I cut my teeth when first betting on-course on horseracing.

It was Bobby Warren, a legend of the East End and part of the Warren boxing family, who helped me from day one at point-to-points giving me my first chance. He was Albert Dimes' right-hand man and like a second father to me. He ran the bookmaking fraternity at some point-to-points in the East of England ensuring the hunts that the bookies who turned up were reputable so all punters got paid.

A story handed down from bookie to bookie from the early 1960s is that the police thought that London gangsters were acting as bookies at one Essex course so they instructed the hunt running the meeting to move the pitches of certain individuals of questionable repute away from the main betting area. Once those bookies had been tipped off what was happening, they broke into the printers and stole the racecards refusing to the hand them over until it was guaranteed that their pitches were back with the others. Turned out the Met were spot on, then.

Also, well back in the day, on an occasion when bookmakers arrived at Little Horwood point-to-point they discovered in horror that a Tote tent had been erected for the first time. Not for long though as

FIFTY YEARS IN THE BETTING JUNGLE

a character called Harry the Horse had an old Tin Lizzy and drove it right through into the next field. Things have changed a lot since then and you can't beat a day at a point-to-point!

Being frank, neither could the bookies when I first started out at the Midlands tracks like Mollington where the Jimmy Tarry horses were the ones to watch, Kingston Blount where Jenny Pidgeon, who was my pin-up girl of point-to-pointing, fared well and Dingley where Jill Dawson used to win all the Ladies' Opens on 1/3 ON favourites. The Dawson horses were unbeatable in Ladies' Opens wherever they went but they hardly ever went hunter chasing with the good ones like Sweet Diana and Roscoe Boy or they would have cleaned up there too.

As for the Essex tracks, Ampton was one of my favourites where David Turner was the king, firstly as a jockey and then as an owner as he used to win everything there. You couldn't lay any of his horses though as they were so hot. He did also happen to own the 4,000 acre farm where Ampton is based.

The reason why bookies couldn't beat a day at a point-to-point back then was because, at the percentages that we were betting to, none of us should have left losing. But now I have to say that's all changed and punters get better value now at point-to-points than they do at racecourses.

Only one bookmaker was allowed to bet on the Grand National and they made hay often betting to over 300% with no hedging facility. Many of the racegoers were just supporting their local hunt and, putting it bluntly, the bookies treated like them like complete wagons when it came to betting. Nowadays they can't get away with it as with more clued-up punters armed with cameras on their mobile

Getting To The Point

phones, it's just one click and the bookie would be shamed all over social media. So the percentages we bet to are now a lot, lot lower than was the case last century but, whatever else you do, a bit of advice, still don't take first show!

I stuck to the Midlands and East Anglia tracks as each point-to-pointing region had their own bookmakers so that no one trod on anyone else's toes. As such I never ventured south of Tweseldown which attracted plenty of the best horses, jockeys and trainers, west of Andoversford, or north of Garthorpe where Joey and Urkie Newton ruled the roost in their famous chocolate colours with Highgate Lady a prolific winner amongst others. One of the bosses of *Dodson & Horrell*, John Sharp, was another standing dish there on the popular Stanwick Lad meeting after meeting, year after year.

***

The biggest meeting of the season is the Melton Hunt Club at Garthorpe which is the pointing equivalent of the Cheltenham Festival and horses venture from all over the land for it unlike for other meetings.

Flying Ace was a winning machine in hunter chases and point-to-points throughout the whole decade of the 1980s. He even won at Mosshouses as a fifteen-year-old in 1991. He had won his last 15 races including nine in the current season before he lined up at Garthorpe in 1985 but, somehow, I managed to get the champion of Scotland beat at 1/5 ON. One Scot had £1,500 to win £300 and gave me the rub up that you only get 10% in the building society but you're giving me 16%.

FIFTY YEARS IN THE BETTING JUNGLE

The judge at Dingley back in the 1980s was notorious for giving dead-heats. It became a standing joke. Obviously, there was no photo-finish system so as long as you had something beaten less than half a length then you still had a fighting chance of drawing. It was hilarious at times.

Cottenham was another of my favourite tracks where they had a fantastic commentator called Hunter Rowe, who was the father of Lisa Hancock who has held top positions in racing including MD of Newmarket and is heavily involved in The Injured Jockeys' Fund. She was another of my pin-up girls. She was also one of the top jockeys on the East Anglian circuit. Hunter was very popular due to his infectious enthusiasm and one day he managed to lock himself inside the commentator's hut as the cars were leaving the course so had to put out a public announcement over the Tannoy for someone to release him.

Spartan Missile is a name that many will best remember chasing home Aldaniti in the 1981 Grand National but to others he was the greatest-ever hunter chaser. It should not be forgotten that he was trying to give Aldaniti and Bob Champion 6lbs including the 3lbs overweight that "54-year-old John Thorne" as Sir Peter O'Sullevan called out in commentary, had put up but they came up four lengths shy.

Back in the late-seventies I saw Spartan Missile run in the second division of the adjacent maiden at Mollington when I was already 'on the chase' so laid an even £1,500 to anyone who wanted to be part of it.

With a circuit to go it was down to a three-horse race but by half-way down the back straight Spartan Missile had gone twenty

Getting To The Point

lengths clear. However, at the fourth-last he hit the top of the fence and slithered on his belly on landing. John Thorne bred him at his nearby farm and also trained and rode him and tried his hardest to lift him up to get him going again having come to a standstill but he couldn't so he had to pull him up.

Spartan Missile went on to win twenty-three of his thirty-eight hunter chases. In fact, *Mackenzie & Selby* rated him as the greatest hunter chaser of all time on 13st having won the Triple Crown of the Cheltenham Foxhunters' by twelve lengths, the Aintree Foxhunters' for a second time having broken a stirrup at half-way on the first occasion and the Horse and Hound Gold Cup at Stratford, so we definitely got away with one in that maiden! Incredibly sadly, Thorne died in a fall at Mollington the year after he was second in the Grand National.

***

I've been luckier than other bookies betting on credit with one major exception. There was one punter that we bookies knew as 'Shorts' as whatever the weather he would turn up in point-to-point betting rings with his knees on show for all to see. He was also a racehorse owner so I let him bet on credit up until the point when it had gone too far with his losses which were now becoming considerable. £228,000 considerable. I let it go that far as I had won fortunes off him so I wanted to keep taking him on.

He had a horse running at the Cheltenham Hunter Chase evening meeting and rang me up to say that he would settle up at the course. All the favourites used to win at that meeting and still do. It's like a ritual every year that as a bookie you have to go and do your bollocks that night.

FIFTY YEARS IN THE BETTING JUNGLE

I was making a book in Tatts when over the Tannoy I heard the dulcet tones of Charlie Parkin: "Would Mr ***** ***** (I'm going to have to keep that to myself I'm afraid) please come to the weighing room. That's a call for Mr ***** *****, would you please come to the weighing room."

I thought, hello, this ain't good. Twenty minutes later and his horse canters past me heading to post wearing a different set of colours, so now all kinds of things are going through my head. The upshot was that I never saw or heard from 'Shorts' ever again and was later told that at one point he loved porridge for breakfast and ended up migrating to live in Asia.

I have been asked if I ever had any enforcers to help bad debtors to pay up as some of my colleagues in the older days did. The answer to that question is no but I always knew people that I could call on if anything got out of hand being due to where I was brought up. I just mentioned Bobby Warren and they would run a mile.

***

As with racecourses there were plenty of characters to be found in the point-to-point betting jungle and some famous names too.

David Jason was often to be seen at Kimble near Aylesbury on Easter Saturdays. I don't know why he kept doing it but when betting with me he'd come up and say: "I'll have twenty quid on all of them, bookie." Did he not know most favourites won at point-to-points? So he was the best punter you can ever have.

I don't know what is it about Kimble but it always seems to attract personalities. Babs Windsor was the Queen of the Carry Ons back in the day and was often seen there and last year Tony Hadley from

Getting To The Point

Spandau Ballet had a bet with me so I got him to autograph my clerk's book. To cut a long story short he lost. He's good but he's no Chas & Dave.

Two well-known faces on the circuit for many years were Clement Freud, the Liberal MP and racing journalist, and his brother, Stephen. Clement wrote about me in one of his columns when giving his views on bookmaking in general and how I would rather be at Cottenham than Newmarket when both were taking place in Cambridgeshire on the same day. He was always a fan of having a sneaky each-way bet against an odds-on favourite.

Jonathan Neesom was Mr Point-to-Point back in the day before he became a *RacingTV* pundit and entertained viewers with his exceptionally-dry sense of humour. He was a very hard man to beat. He used to produce a form guide which was considered as the weekly pointing bible which I subscribed to. *Mackenzie And Selby's Point-to-Pointers and Hunter Chasers* was the annual bible that didn't pull any punches when it came to describing the merits of bad horses and even worse jockeys.

***

Tweseldown was one of the first courses that I stood at and also one of the great point-to-point tracks having been a former jumps course up until 1932 when it hosted the Grand Military Gold Cup before it moved to Sandown and equestrian events at the London Olympics in 1948. It closed down for racing in 2012 which was a sad day for the sport. I made sure I was there that day to say goodbye.

I was also at Tweseldown when it played host to the first Sunday racing with legal betting in 1996 and the local vicar gave a sermon for about twenty minutes in the freezing cold before the first. When Cheltenham held the first ever Sunday race day four years earlier when the highlight was Granville Again beating his brother Morley Street, both of which won a Champion Hurdle, no on-course betting was allowed so I thought fuck that!

When I appeared as a guest on *Luck On Sunday* a few years back Nick told me that when he struck his first ever bet, there was a very good chance that it was me at Tweseldown when he was about nine. I would have made sure his mum and dad were in attendance. ;-)

One of my favourite point-to-pointers was Ross Poldark ridden by Ian and later Clare Balding and he was a regular at Tweseldown. Even though the Royal trainer was still a top operator in 1982 and for many years to follow, he loved to ride in point-to-points at the same time and his dream was to win the Aintree Foxhunters'. Ian recounts this story in his autobiography and I can confirm every word of it as I was the bookie he referred to that got hit for two grand, by his Gold Cup, Champion Hurdle and Grand National-winning brother, Toby Balding no less!

I opened up 20/1 for Ross Poldark for an Open race at the Army Meeting for the first run of his life at the age of……..eleven! That is not a misprint. Toby asked Ian what on earth he was doing running him in an Open rather than a maiden and making a certainty of it, only to be told that the horse was working better than a novice hurdler that had recently won at Taunton even with Ian as the work rider so he must have also been giving that horse two stone on the gallops. Toby didn't waste any time having £100 on with me after I had gone

Getting To The Point

up with my first show and by off-time, sustained support saw him go off at close to Evens. It must have won by a hundred yards.

After Ross Poldark won a few more Open races at Tweseldown, Ian did get his big chance of winning over the Grand National fences as he was also on top when they started favourite for the Aintree Foxhunters' the following season. However, he came up short finishing fourth in a small field having led until the final fence after he had starved himself for weeks to make the weight as jockeys carry more weight in point-to-points. *Mackenzie & Selby* wrote that Ross Poldark was too small for the Aintree fences. As for the winner, that was Atha Cliath which probably means nothing to most of us but he was ridden by an amateur jockey by the name of Mr W P Mullins. I wonder whatever became of him?

As a bookmaker, when the jockey is younger than the horse, that's generally a sign to lay the bollocks off it! That was the case when Clare Balding and Ross Poldark were both aged sixteen when Clare had her first ride in a point-to-point at Hackwood Park so she was put on a very safe jumper. As much as I loved that horse, in those circumstances I just had to lay it. Little did I know that many years later I would be working with Clare on the BBC.

Also riding in the race was another big trainer's daughter, Amanda Harwood, and they fought it out with the now Amanda Perrett just getting the verdict. On the grass standing in between our pitches was Robin Gray commentating who loved a drink but no one could see what was going on with bouncy castles and all the fun of the fair, in which case he always went to his go-to line of "It's a Battle Royale" as no one could see the finish.

FIFTY YEARS IN THE BETTING JUNGLE

Despite winning the Derby, Eclipse, King George and Arc with Mill Reef, Balding wrote: "I do not think I was ever happier in my life than when bowling along in front making the running on him (Ross Poldark) in those point-to-points at Tweseldown." Even though he did cost me dear that one time, I too was very fond of the old bugger. Ross not Ian. Also, this is incontrovertible proof that bad jump racing is better than top class flat racing. Toby would have agreed with that.

***

As this chapter header says, if you have never done so, get yourself to a point-to-point, it really is a great family day out with a picnic and a punt. You'll see more Fortnum & Mason hampers here than you do at Fortnum & Mason and more Range Rovers than in the plant at Solihull

Obviously, I've slowed down somewhat and like my warmth now more than in the early days but you can still find me at Kimble on Easter Saturday with my Zeiss bins looking for film stars (we miss you Babs) plus various other points including at High Easter near Chelmsford. Two years ago, I couldn't believe my mince pies when a legend of the betting ring Victor Chandler was there and came up with his son and had £20 on with me. Now there was a bookmaker who dressed like bookmakers should dress. Immaculate. He wrote an autobiography last year called *Put Your Life On It*.

Why do I still bet at point-to-points? It was how I was brought up with Mikey Falco and the Warren family. Even now it still brings back memories of the old days and seeing their families still there.

Sharon says that I can't write this but I'm going to anyway. All the women look the same in their *Favour and Fairfax* boots and *Holland*

Getting To The Point

Cooper jackets, they just have different heads. Point-to-points haven't only been a breeding ground for horses, jockeys and trainers though but also where clothing companies like *Joules* started out and, being serious, most people look fantastic in their country wear. Makes you feel proud to be British.

And I can't not mention the German sausage man. His frankfurters cut in half with his huge silver knife have kept me going on many a cold day.

So, if you see me at a point-to-point, come on up and say hello and help old Gal out with a few bets. I'll even sign this book for you! My favourite callout to try and drag punters in now is 'Bet with the TV bookie as you all know me. I eat all the quarter pounders on the McDonalds adverts.'

6
Hitting The Fairways

The only betting shop that I have ever owned was in partnership with Del Burrows in the small market town of Raunds in Northamptonshire. Previous to that it was a Cobblers, which the county was best known for, and you must think what is to follow is cobblers but I can assure you that it was all one hundred per cent true.

We only employed one member of staff, my stepson Grant, but we hardly got any business being based in such a quiet place so it was one of the worst decisions I made but we had a three-year lease that we couldn't get out of. The only busy day we had every year was Grand National Day but it kept Grant in a job. I mainly turned up when Del Boy and me fancied a game of snooker before the dogs.

I was licenced under the name of Fairway Bookmakers and right behind our office was a snooker hall. There was one young lad aged about nine or ten who used to practice there who often came into our shop before the racing started with his dad. We let him sit behind the counter and gave him some pop and sweets. His name was Shaun Murphy.

In his early-twenties this kid from the neighbouring village of Irthlingborough only then went and won the World

FIFTY YEARS IN THE BETTING JUNGLE

Championship at his first attempt in 2005. I'd like to think that my advice helped get him there! "Whenever you get a chance, son, tuck 'em up." Quite the opposite as he proceeded to pot his opponents off the table.

How he hasn't become world champion again in twenty years since then given what a magician he is with a cue in his hands, I really don't know as outside Ronnie O'Sullivan and Judd Trump he must be the most naturally gifted player I've seen.

Like me he had gastric sleeve surgery a couple of years ago having lost his self-esteem, confidence and also his form on the green baize but since then he has looked a different animal both on and off the snooker table. It's turned his life around, basically. In the final two weeks of this book going to print he's just won the Masters so there is time to win a second world title yet.

Another regular visitor to my betting office was David Dickinson. No, not the cheap-as-chips orange one with the magnificent head of hair bargain hunter but the BHA Handicapper for two-mile hurdlers up until recent years, who lived in Raunds. Whilst holding that position he was obviously not allowed to bet but years earlier when he was working for *Raceform* as one of their handicappers, he landed a huge payout in 1989 when playing the high numbers in the Dick Peacock Sprint at Thirsk where the highest-drawn trio finished 1-2-3 at 20/1, 25/1 and 33/1.

There was a big draw bias back then but as it was in the days when such stats weren't readily available pre-internet, those who had cottoned onto it were taking advantage at Thirsk and other tracks like Ripon, Nottingham and Folkestone for years. David was one

Hitting The Fairways

such punter and the tricast paid around £14K to a £1 unit. All I can say is this, thank God my shop didn't open until a few years later or he would have cleaned me out that day!

When he arrived at my office before racing started, on the rare occasions when I was also there, we used to pull up our stools together and have a good, long chat putting the world to rights. He kept having the same draw-combination bets with us and did more than alright but nothing close to the extent of his big win. Now that David has retired, he is back punting again but on French racing mainly as he thinks there's a better edge there and specialises in cross-country chases.

To this day I have kept the licence for Fairway Bookmakers. When we sold up, you'll never guess who took over the premises? Con Wilson who we had the Norton's Coin bet with!

***

Onto a different kind of fairway and many of you will already be aware of the Hole-In-One Gang, a couple of seriously-wised-up Essex lads with a background in the betting industry who in the early-nineties got the better of managers of independent betting shops up and down the country asking for and getting up to 100/1 about a hole-in-one in any given tournament when the true odds were nearer even money.

What you will be unaware of is that I was at it a couple of years before they landed their big pay day with Johhny Earl. I say 'I' but he was the brains behind it. I told you that he was the cleverest man I knew.

Where the Essex boys were really clever was that back in 1991, before golf betting properly began to take off, they put in the research and identified the five biggest tournaments where an ace was statistically odds-on so also placed doubles, trebles and accumulators. All five won and they cleaned up winning over half a million.

They also travelled far and wide to get the bets on whereas we just kept it local to near where the golf tournament was taking place to make the story of why we wanted the bet seem more genuine. We wanted to give the impression that we were such keen golf followers that we were attending the event, even though I had never held a golf club in anger. I even wore a Slazenger jersey when entering the shops which I thought was a nice touch! It wasn't easy to find one in my size but we managed it.

It had to be done with the independents though as they could do what they liked rather than have to ring up head office for clearance as then the bigger firms would probably have smelt a rat. We'd get chatting first, all pally-like trying to work the manager out, whether they might be clueless on golf or not?

We had to be careful regarding stakes though as most of these independent betting offices had a notice on the wall outlining a maximum payout of £10,000 amongst many other T&Cs. Anyway, on the first occasion we weren't careful. We won £5,000 and thought, hello, we're onto something here, especially as we had also doubled and trebled it up with other big tournaments in the coming weeks.

That successful bet was placed in Salisbury where the independent betting shop owner, who also had a side business of supplying condoms to machines in pubs, then worked it out before we came to collect our winnings on the single bet that his liabilities on the doubles and trebles came into serious thousands. He didn't have one of those

Hitting The Fairways

notice boards on display so there was no maximum payout but at the same time we quickly realised that if all three won then there was just no way he could pay, so the three of us sat down and played our own version of *Deal Or No Deal* with JE as Noel Edmonds.

On top of the five grand that we had already won we agreed on eight more for him to get out of it and call the bets off. A few years later he came up to my pitch at Bath and asked if I remembered him? I didn't remember the face but I certainly remembered the story so shook him by the hand!

Talking of *Deal or No Deal*, I'd love to take that Banker on and tell him what he really should be offering knowing what the true odds are!

I was close to being on an ITV show called *The Colour of Money* hosted by Chris Tarrant as their banker but they went for an attractive, young lady instead. I can't imagine why! They had sent me down to be fitted at Saville Row and were pleased with all the rehearsals but then I got the chop at the last minute. So at least Matt Chapman lasted for one more edition than me before he was sacked from *Dancing On Ice*! You know we love you Matt!

***

When shops had board markers, Jackson & Lowe used to send out the horseracing betting sheets to the independents. They also sent one on for The Open Championship in 1988 at Lytham St Anne's with the odds already listed that was posted to arrive on Tuesdays.

Also on that sheet was Group Betting and Match Betting but no Hole-In-One Betting so we spotted an opportunity. It was then organised that we copied the betting sheet to look as close to the original, and it was almost identical, and would send it out to arrive

FIFTY YEARS IN THE BETTING JUNGLE

to the independents on the Monday in the Midlands area that we were concentrating on but sneaking on a Hole-In-One section where 'No' was 1/33 and 'Yes' was 25/1. Therefore, when then real sheets arrived a day later, they would get dumped in the bin. By law, on our betting sheet we had to have our name of Fairway Bookmakers with our phone number listed just in case anyone wanted to hedge, and one did.

So once they were on display in various Midlands independents, we set about getting on and opted for small stakes in lots of shops driving from town to town over the course of the next two days. Derby was a particularly good area as had lots of independents.

I drove up to Royal Lytham & St Annes on the Thursday morning arriving at the course at 10am and, wouldn't you know it, when I looked up at the giant yellow scoreboard there was already a red one on it as Lanny Wadkins had made an ace. Johnny had done his research beforehand and found out that Lytham's Par 3s were considered to be more likely to produce a hole-in-one than other courses on the Open roster so we had picked the right year. In the three Opens held at Lytham since, there has been a hole-in-one at two of them.

Seve Ballesteros went on to win in a first-ever Monday finish beating Nick Price and Nick Faldo but I was already back at home and celebrating by Thursday night!

We debated whether we should try it again the following year but decided that once was enough to pull off this stroke. A one-off, a one-round O'Reilly. Like my mum's home-made apple pie and custard, we only dared to try it once.

7
Owning It

I loved the old Jim Joel colours. Remember them? All black with a scarlet cap. So classy and best remembered by many when carried by Royal Palace to win the 2000 Guineas and Derby in 1967.

He was trained by Noel Murless and ridden by the Aussie, George Moore, but a setback ruled him out of going for the Triple Crown. He was even better as a four-year-old winning the Coronation Cup, Prince of Wales's Stakes, Eclipse and King George and Queen Elizabeth Diamond Stakes in less than two months under Sandy Barclay. Unfortunately, he did a leg in the home straight when gamely hanging on at Ascot so had to be retired straight afterwards.

Not only that but Maori Venture won the Grand National twenty years later for Jim at the grand old age of ninety-two. Loads of people couldn't have him on their minds saying that he was the worst jumper in the race beforehand but under Steve Knight for Andy Turnell his class came through winning at 28/1. It's interesting to see how the race has changed since then as only eleven of the forty horses were in the handicap and thirty-two were aged in double figures including the first six. It's a very different race now with hardly any geriatrics and first and second-season chasers dominating as of late.

FIFTY YEARS IN THE BETTING JUNGLE

Being the only set of racing colours to pass the post in front in both the Derby and Grand National, and Royal Palace being one of the horses that got me hooked on racing and betting, I was in no doubt, I wanted a set of colours as close to his that Weatherbys would allow. I managed to get black with navy blue epaulettes and red cap. The dog's bollocks. Not bad if I say so myself!

***

I've touched on this story before but it's a good 'un and have added more meat to the bone.

Vado Via is an Italian phrase which translates as 'I'm Leaving' and that's what we did with over fifty grand in readies after we landed a right touch on her in a conditional jockeys' handicap hurdle at Haydock in November of 1992. However, it was only in the nick of time that we arrived at the course at all to get the readies down.

For Vado Via's previous race, we had booked Miss Claire Balding claiming 7lbs. No, not the one from the *Revitive* adverts, though she has been known to do other things(!), but a different one with an 'i' that David Wintle had put up. They finished fourth on the flat over 1m4f at Leicester in a big field as a 25/1 outsider which set up our four-year-old filly very nicely for this three-mile handicap hurdle. We didn't care that she was racing from 7lbs out of the handicap as knew how good she was but that disadvantage obviously helped with us getting a bigger price.

Warren Marston was due to ride and set to take off 5lbs. Alongside the trainer and my driver that day Gary Selby, we all headed up the M6 in the same car only to run into another one of its massive traffic jams in Staffordshire.

Owning It

I don't know how Gary got us there but we entered the betting ring at 2.06pm with the race set to start at 2.10pm. Actually, I do know how as he ignored all the signs and used the hard shoulder before taking the back roads aided by something called a road map (for any younger readers you can Google what one of them is) and dropped us off outside the front gates as the car park was too far away as they were already on their way to post and I was hardly built like Linford Christie.

But before all of that, we knew that there was no chance of Wazza getting there in time to weigh out so we had to sort a replacement pronto. This wasn't as easy as it sounds as firstly there were no mobile phones back then and, secondly, it had to be a conditional jockey of course. So, we stopped off at a service station and David got on the blower to the weighing room to see who was available.

Luckily for us there was just one conditional rider at the course that didn't already have a ride in the race so Finbar Murtagh was booked on the spot, otherwise we would have been forced to withdraw the filly. As mentioned earlier, Wazza was set to claim 5lbs which was helping to offset Vado Via being out of the handicap but as Finbar had ridden more winners, he couldn't claim any weight off so that was going to make our task harder. What other choice did we have though except to take her out of the race? Twister had the odds-on jolly ridden by David Bridgwater who later went on to train for me who also couldn't claim in this race, so at least that was something.

The riding instructions from that service station to Finbar were along the lines of, this is a very long home straight with a very long run-in so, whatever else you do, don't let her go until she jumps the last and she'll win.

The one bonus about being very late was that the 4/1 we were expecting turned out to be 7/1 as there was no money for her as we hadn't arrived yet, so into action I sprang. Two grand on with Tom James of Doncaster (real name Raymond Geraghty from a long-standing bookmaking family) and the same stake with Leslie Steele of Leeds who made it to over one hundred years of age and then Pat Whelan aka The Fifth Beatle just because he was from Liverpool and finally Graham Liles from Leeds at the back whose son Richard has taken over the family business and is the president of the British Racecourse Bookmakers' Association.

Once the race started the first two-and-a-half miles went perfectly to plan as Vado Via was held up in rear. I was heading back to the stands to watch the finish and then all of a sudden, I heard the commentor call out: "Entering the straight and Vado Via has now hit the front and gone four lengths clear." What!? There were still three flights to jump up that long, unforgiving home straight.

Thankfully she held on and in the post-race debrief Finbar said that she was going so well that he just couldn't hold on any longer. This was comfortably my biggest win on any of the horses I have ever owned.

The Vado Via story didn't end there though. Not by a long chalk. As horses can't be penalised for winning a conditional jockeys' race, we quickly took advantage of that and got her out twice more in the next six days where she went on to win under Wazza at Nottingham on ITV's *World Of Sport* and then again for Warren Jenks at Newton

Owning It

Abbot but we just enjoyed those successes for what they were with no major bets.

She ran off a handicap mark of 100 when winning at Haydock and two months later she was rated a career-high of 129 to underline just how well handicapped David Wintle had got her. It's when you have your biggest edges that you should have your biggest stakes.

Three seasons later Wazza went on to have a fantastic Cheltenham Festival winning the Supreme Novice on the outsider Indefence and Sun Alliance Chase on Nahthen Lad, both for Jenny Pitman. David Wintle was a shrewd man and great character who died in 2017 after training over 350 winners. As for Vado Via, see my next tale.

***

When Vado Via retired, I decided to breed from her. The result of sending her to Sure Blade to be covered at Aston Park Stud was that she became the dam of the best horse that I ever owned called Mi Odds, named after my car registration plate.

We put him in training with Norma Macauley who was the hardest woman I ever met but I loved her to bits. I lost count of the number of kids she had and her father was Norman Scobie who trained in the north.

Mi Odds kept progressing to the extent that he was fancied for the Winter Derby at Lingfield in 2001 having won at Southwell the previous month. Shortly afterwards I got a fax through from a bloodstock agent in America offering £150,000 for him. I wanted to take it but Norma said when he wins the Winter Derby he will be worth £300,000. Unfortunately, he had a setback and missed the race. How's your fucking luck?

FIFTY YEARS IN THE BETTING JUNGLE

When I thought Mi Odds was nearing the end of his career with Norma, I wanted to bring him closer to home as I was living in Windy Ridge which was practically on Ian Williams' gallops in Alvechurch. By the way I recommend the doughnuts from the fabulous Becketts Farm Shop just up the road. Different class.

So I moved him to Ian who suggested that we give him a run in a seller at Hereford which would be his first time over hurdles so he was well schooled beforehand. With the help of fellow bookie Tom Fruit (real first name and he used to sell fruit in a Leicester market), somehow we managed to get Mi Odds opened up at 4/1 before smashing him into 9/4. On his flat form he should have been odds-on and we knew that he had schooled well. In the race he pulled like stink over a longer trip against slower horses so in the end he had to be driven out by David Dennis but he won by just over a length. Lovely.

After five more runs for Ian over hurdles where he didn't win again, we then sent him back to Norma to go flat racing again for the better prize money and she managed to get four more wins out of him over the next seven months before he was claimed after winning at Wolverhampton. During his career he ran over one hundred times and won fifteen races. What an absolute superstar he was.

***

One of my best days as an owner was when we landed a very nice double on Montague Dawson at Southwell and Kemys Commander at Market Rasen.

Mark Johnson was commentating when the Commander won and I still dream about his call: "Kemys Commander carrying the colours

Owning It

of bookie Gary Wiltshire and Norma Macauley are going to land an across-the-card double." It sounded absolutely fantastic.

However, it also likely caused Norma's divorce! She hadn't told her husband Donald that this double had been the plan for a while and he was with me at Market Rasen when Stormin' Norman brought the Commander home in the second leg. Prior to his victory I had told Donald that I was off to the betting shop to watch Monty run and he said don't bother, Norma says it's useless.

Putting two and two together after both horses had won Donald quicky realised that we had had it right off with the double. I know it's not exactly Barney Curley territory with his four-horse plan that took him over two years to piece together but it was a job well done. Norma and Donald went their separate ways a couple of months later.

***

In addition to David, Norma, Ian and Bridgy, I have had horses with Joe Naughton, Tony Carroll, Patrick Chamings, David Evans, Seamus Mullins, Nikki Evans, Richard Phillips, Ali Stronge and Tony Newcombe. When any of them said to me we needed to stick some blinkers on, that wasn't because they were flying! So, I've had it my head ever since and never wanted to be with a horse wearing headgear......like Fujiyama Crest. TC never let you down. He rode horses for me before training them.

The saddest day of my racing life was when Richard Davis died of his injuries from a fall at Southwell in 1996. He rode in my colours on a few occasions and really was a smashing, good-looking young man who had the rest of his life in front of him. A sharp reminder of the dangers involved in the sport that we love. His name lives on as part of the JETS charity set up to help former and current professional jockeys achieve a secure future with their annual awards named in his honour.

Stormin' Norman Williamson was the jockey that I always wanted when we were trying to land a touch as, to my eyes, he was the best back then. We didn't get him that often as he wanted to be on good horses! He was one of a select few jockeys to win the Champion Hurdle and Gold Cup in the same season on Alderbrook and Master Oats, both for Kim Bailey in 1995.

Call me Mr Ambitious but we ran Old Road from 68lbs out of the handicap against Jodami at Haydock who had won the Cheltenham Gold Cup earlier that year! Has there ever been a horse any more out of the handicap than that!? We were only after third-place prize money in that three-runner race so booked Chris Grant for the first time as Rambo was the man to get a horse round Haydock.

I used to deal with Matt Chapman when he was Darryl Holland's agent who was easy to get along with, even though he later nicked my job on Sky greyhounds! We remained good mates ever since and you can't beat him and Nick Luck as TV presenters. If I was allowed an ante-post fiver on the next face of racing, I'll go with ex-*Love Island* contestant Frankie Foster who loves the game inside out. Just a shame he's not as good looking as me.

***

Back in 1993 I ran my own advisory service which was advertised in *The Sporting Life*. Once punters registered with us, around two

Owning It

hundred of them with a waiting list of another ton, the way it worked was that they would put £40 on each selection for me and if it won then send the money to P O Box 717, Keyworth Post Office, south of Nottingham.

My clients included none other than the legendary Mancunian comedian Bernard Manning and the not-so-legendary light-entertainment star Joe Longthorne plus a couple in their sixties, the Bakers from Guernsey, who we found out were having absolute bundles on.

Some of the info we got on horses and dogs was top drawer to the extent that we even had nineteen consecutive winning days, not selections, so we were raking it in. The way it worked was that Sharon rang them up individually. Sounds like a hell of a task but the calls would only last about ten seconds with, name, time, place, done and they all knew their fifteen-minutes' time slot so to be ready.

On May 13th 1994 we had our best day when a horse of mine called Greek Night Out, who I claimed out of Mark Johnston's stable and ran in Sharon's name, landed a touch from 20/1 into 8/1 at Nottingham for Norma Macauley ridden by Jimmy Fortune. We advised all our clients to take the first show. If the horse had ran in my name, it would more likely have opened up at 5/1.

When Sharon went to collect the cheques and postal orders a few days later, there was only between sixty-seventy envelopes. Turns out over half of our clients were very happy sending back money when backing shorter-priced winners but were not so keen when it came to sending back £800! We learned a lesson that day never to put up big prices again and, obviously having lost their trust, those who failed to pay up never got another call.

Most did pay up when we landed a similar punt from 14s into 7s a few months earlier when Stormin' Norman won a seller at Nottingham on another of my horses Tynron Doon but we didn't stipulate first show on that occasion.

I consoled myself that between my own bets and those who did pay up after Greek Night Out's win that I ended up winning almost £250,000. With those winnings we bought a bungalow in Stanton-on-the-Wolds and called it Sebley as Sharon's amateur jockey name was Miss S E Broadley.

As over half of our members decided to welch on the deal, not long after we changed our plan to setting up an 0898 number service where I left the message. That too was going well until I made a massive error of judgement.

In short, there was a three-runner race at Fontwell and I owned the favourite. It must have been a bad race as he was next to useless as he had loads of issues so I recommended a reverse forecast on the other two and also to back them in win singles. Although my horse was the morning favourite, it drifted on course to be the outsider of three and the market proved to be spot on so the forecast copped.

The following morning, I got a phone call from a big cheese in the racing authorities who said: "Gary, you've got a good name but if you don't suspend this service immediately, action WILL be taken." I decided to take his advice. Hands up, I did wrong.

***

Owning It

Those were tales that went our way but obviously many others went tits up. In gambling it's usually when you need it most when you don't win.

I never bought horses from the sales so it was all via sellers and claimers with my own eyes. One time when it didn't go my way was at Nottingham where there was a horse which I really liked that won the claimer by 3½l for Chris Wall and ridden by Philip Robinson. So, I put in a claim for it at £6,000.

There was just one other claim for her and back in those days it was then pure luck who would get it as there was a bag with two balls inside and whoever pulled out the ball with number one written on it got the horse. I delved my hand inside the bag first and I pulled out the two ball.

She was called Mysilv and nine months later she went on to win the Triumph Hurdle. What an absolute choker.

8
The Cheltenham Rollercoaster

Funny thing about the Cheltenham Festival, when bookies walk through the gates, they suddenly grow a pair of bollocks. It's amazing. For 51 weeks of the year, they are as meek as lambs these days but come the second week of March they suddenly decide they want to become a bookie and do have an opinion after all and stick their neck out. So, here's four Cheltenham Festival betting ring anecdotes from which I survived to tell the tale, one that went against me and three where I somehow came out smelling of roses when all looked lost on a couple of occasions.

***

Ask any bookmaker and most will have an Annie Power tale to tell so here's mine. It was a glorious day for the start of the 2015 Cheltenham Festival with not just excitement and fevered anticipation in the air but also clear, bright, blue skies and, who knows, that is what might have come to save us bookies that day?

Having the favourites for the four Grade 1 races on the Tuesday, Willie Mullins and Ruby Walsh were expected to have a very good day. On what was being called 'Ruby Tuesday' in all the build up after The Rolling Stones song, they were not just the favourites but very strong favs at that as none were bigger than bottle, 2/1. For punters to try and make some proper mileage, rather than betting them as win-only singles, the accas and Lucky 15s poured in up and down the land in Britain and Ireland so if all four copped then it would have paid around 12/1 so the off-course liabilities were huge.

The horse that betting firms most placed their faith in getting beat was Douvan being the only one of the four not to be priced up at odds-on. Therefore, they must have already been fearing the worst when he won the Supreme Novices' Hurdle comfortably at 2/1. This was shortly followed by Un De Sceaux making all to run away with the Arkle who was returned at 4/6 and his backers never had a moment's worry either.

So now it was officially squeaky-bum time for the big firms and their mood took an even greater turn for the worse when all the other jockeys decided to gift Walsh a freebie from the outset on Faugheen in the Champion Hurdle, so that race was as good as over after just one flight with Ruby dictating as he pleased on the 4/5 fav making all.

Now the alarm bells were well and truly ringing in Barking, Leeds, Stoke, Warrington, Wigan, Harrow, Dublin and Gibraltar. It wouldn't have been as bad for them as Dettori Day if Annie Power won as the combined odds at Ascot were 25,095/1 at SP (and massively bigger for anyone who took morning prices as I don't need reminding that Fujiyama Crest was 16/1 before racing started and ended up at 2s) but not far off as ALL punters bet on the Cheltenham Festival unlike what is now Champions Day at Ascot so there were floods of bets on this accumulator.

The Cheltenham Rollercoaster

So, it was all rolling onto Annie Power in the Mares' Hurdle and the firms were staring into the abyss at a collective loss of anything between £40-100 million depending on which bookie reps you listened to afterwards. The bigger the loss, the bigger the story and publicity for them so it was much more likely to have been at the lower end of those estimates.

The first bet I laid was £30K to win £20K at 4/6 from the Magic Sign, Ladbrokes, as all their reps were running round the ring backing it to reduce their liabilities, so they did a good job as she went off at 1/2 ON. You don't get that now as the bigger firms hedge on the exchanges as barely any send reps to the racecourse anymore.

A year earlier Annie Power was the beaten favourite when she didn't stay three miles in the Stayers' Hurdle against the boys so there was still some hope for the bookies but this race was over two-and-a-half miles and back against fellow mares.

As an on-course bookie, I hadn't taken any accumulators so that side of things wasn't personally affecting me but I was still around ten large down after the first four races with the other Mullins hotpots doing the business. So, the old Gary burst back into life as I saw it as an opportunity to stand Annie Power at an artificially-short price given all the liabilities running onto her so stood her to get it all back in one go.

One of my big pals is Ralph Peters, the owner of Slush Puppie who at the last count have sold over two billion cups of the neon-bright sweet stuff, was working with me that day in that he had a financial interest in the book. He loved a gamble and wouldn't let me take the best odds that we were offering off the board, which I was more than happy with. So, with the help of our outside man Stefan from Belgium who was telling us who was pricing up what nearby, we kept going biggest standing at my back-row pitch in Tatts.

Once the race started Ruby had the hot favourite settled in touch just off the pace and only started to make his move from three out. Taking it up at the second-last, it already looked a question of how far as Annie Power was four lengths to the good and going best heading to the final hurdle. Obviously she had it won so in despair I had already turned my back only to hear a massive gasp from the first-day, record crowd who had reached fever pitch just a few strides earlier as all she had to do was clear the last and immediately I knew that I was saved.

I couldn't believe it but these are the things that make the Cheltenham Festival great as here we are talking about it a decade later as if it happened yesterday and we still will be well into the future.

It was a bad-looking fall at that but thankfully both horse and jockey were fine. She just took off a stride too soon throwing herself at the hurdle, clipped the top and came down. Mullins said that she was "probably going too well" which doubtless cheered her backers up no end! A year later she won the Champion Hurdle. Her owner Rich Ricci very recently told us that Annie Power winning the Champion Hurdle was the best moment that he has ever had in racing especially given what had happening the previous year.

It was the cruellest blow for those punters who had it all riding on her so, for some bookies to be seen celebrating basically rubbing their faces in it, I thought that was terrible. They can think it, and let's be

The Cheltenham Rollercoaster

brutally honest we all did, but show some respect and don't show it. It was a very eerie five minutes that followed. Mullins still won the race with Glens Melody but it was a lovely old skinner for the books.

I'll never forget we had a friend of the family called Billy who was a smashing fella and a real racing man who was on the accumulator and he came up to see me ashen-faced after the race looking like a ghost. He was clearly in pain after such a twist of fate. At least those punters with Lucky 15s could still console themselves with a decent pick-up from their outlay.

Betting next to us that day was the Welsh bookmaker John Lovell whose sons David and James went on to form the internet betting firm DragonBet and he be would proud of them. He died tragically in a car accident on a roundabout when a lorry driver took it too fast and ended up on top of his car killing him instantly. We dearly miss you, pal.

Oddly enough it was a case of déjà vu four years later when Benie Des Dieux had an identical fall in the same race at the same flight also for Mullins, Walsh and Ricci having also raced into a clear lead heading to the last when she was considered the dreaded 'Festival Banker' of the week. I used to love taking on the 'Festival Banker' as we got most of them beat, often some slow old boat from Ireland in the Four-Miler, so it was only dreaded from a punter's point of view.

The one thing I will say is this. It was a very sunny day both years so maybe that had something to do with it with the race taking place after 4pm. So was it the low sun that saved the bookies' skins? Some have suggested more sinister tactics were at play after the Ile De Chypre stun-gun affair or whatever you want to call it. Who knows, but the Annie Power story will forever go down in Cheltenham Festival and gambling folklore.

***

Apart from family I have only had two regular clerks down the years and but also a few stand-ins including Max Weatherby, the son of Johnny Weatherby whose company published this book and have such a great name in the racing game. The first was Gary Selby who I met in a Coral shop in Milton Keynes and was working on the American racing for *Attheraces* at the time and the second was Peter Houghton who was previously a chef from Torquay.

It was Peter who saved me on the first day of the 2002 Cheltenham Festival which, I am afraid Ruby Walsh, is a third mention about you falling at the last hurdle when about to win! I should point out that Ruby did win a record 59 races at the meeting from Alexander Banquet in the Weatherbys Champion Bumper in 1998 to Klassical Dream in the Supreme in 2019 and was a class apart.

In the opening Supreme Novices' Hurdle, we had stood the J P McManus-owned, short-priced favourite ridden by Charlie Swan called Like-A-Butterfly to lose £27K on the lower rails. Why? How many eight-year-old mares win novice hurdles at the Cheltenham Festival? This was also back in the days when there were massive fields so I wanted to take her on in a 28-runner race to try and make a flying start to the week. Reading that back, I should have stood for her for even more!

The Cheltenham Rollercoaster

Despite the huge field, from three out only five mattered having gone clear of the pack and Ruby on the 12/1 chance Adamant Approach was taking dead aim at Charlie racing directly behind him, who was sat in second and was poised to challenge a ridden-along Westender owned by a pal of mine from the flower market in Birmingham called Matt Archer with Jean Broadhurst in the Aston Villa colours. Matt always had a large cigar and looks exactly what a racehorse owner should look like.

On the outside Adamant Approach's white blaze had just nosed its way into the lead at the last flight which was parallel to where I was standing so I had a front row seat for the drama about to unfold. The horse must have thought he was a tank as he ran straight into the hurdle barely raising a leg and upon hitting the deck he hampered Native Scout who certainly wasn't out of it in third place. This left the mare a couple of lengths clear.

Whilst all the favourite backers cheered like crazy when she was left in front, there was one big collective groan from the bookies. We still had a chance though as McCoy was coming again on the second-favourite Westender for Pipey who was rallying but they couldn't quite get there and went down by a neck.

It was the worst possible start and I stood it for every pound in my pocket. Not only were we potless for the rest of the day but also the rest of the festival so although we then continued to bet on the second race, the Arkle, it would have been a case of borrowing money off any other bookie if we lost on that race as well. It's an unwritten rule that this is what bookies do for each other.

FIFTY YEARS IN THE BETTING JUNGLE

But still, that wouldn't be enough to see us into Day 2 so I left the racecourse straight after the first and caught a taxi to the town centre to visit as many banks as I could to draw out enough readies to play with on the Wednesday and left Peter to man the joint and continue taking bets. I managed to draw out £15,000 between them and still had time to watch Moscow Flyer beat the Pipe/McCoy favourite Seebald for the Liverpool duo of Robbie Fowler and Steve McManaman in a Coral.

Walking back to the cab rank to head back to the course, when passing one of the pubs I got pulled in by legendary Irish face Patsy Byrne and his family including Willie and Nolan and a legend of the Irish betting ring known as Spike plus plenty more of Barney Curley's pals to join them to watch the Champion Hurdle. Within minutes, that £15K which I had just drawn out? I had only laid to lose all of it on Istabraq taking a fifteen grand to eight. Actually it was in Euros so not quite all.

Istabraq was going for what would have been an unprecedented fourth win in the race but I thought surely Peter has got to have laid it too. He was now aged ten and missed his big chance of getting to four Champion Hurdle wins the previous year when the meeting was abandoned due to Foot and Mouth. Well, we know what happened, he was pulled up after only two hurdles by Charlie Swan who was clearly under instructions from Aidan O'Brien that if he was not happy with him then to take no chances. He had gone lame.

After the race though, the Irish lads wouldn't let me go. They wanted the Dettori story all over again and I still have to tell them the same tale when we meet up in a London pub for what is now an annual tradition on the Thursday of Cheltenham including my stepson,

The Cheltenham Rollercoaster

Liam. They know how to treat someone with a day's wages. God bless you Patsy, we miss you and your boys do you a great honour.

As for the rest of that Tuesday card, I ended £20K up in the pub and, not only that, Peter had turned it round completely on the track so in the end we had a blinding day.

***

It's not often a horse beaten in its previous race goes off 2/1 favourite for the Weatherbys Champion Bumper. But that's what happened in 2003 when Liberman won for Martin Pipe, AP McCoy and David Johnson.

Mind you, that defeat was a close-up second four months earlier to Rhinestone Cowboy who the previous day started favourite for the Champion Hurdle as a novice and finished third to Rooster Booster. So Liberman was all the rage for the finale on what was the middle day of three back then.

I was already 'on the chase' as the bookies call it being £50K down on the day mainly thanks to a big plunge on Tony Martin's Xenophon from 8/1 into 4/1 favourite for the Coral Cup. He was the shrewdest trainer around at that time with a reputation for landing big gambles. Mick Fitz rode it and afterwards he let it be known that he had told Martin it was a cert having also won a big handicap on him at Leopardstown two months earlier. Like all the bookies, we got heavily hit by that.

Moscow Flyer winning his first Champion Chase about half an hour earlier also didn't help matters so we stood Liberman to lose around £50K to try and get half our losses back. I should be on *The Chase* with Bradley Walsh given the a mount of times that's been the case down the years. When we go to Hemsby we often drop in at Bradley's brother's Del Boy Café which gives you the biggest all-day breakfasts you can eat.

Punters couldn't get enough of Liberman, especially with it being in the getting-out stakes for those who were behind and, being Pipe and McCoy, the winning punters on the day were playing up their winnings after Moscow Flyer and Xenophon. David Johnson didn't back him with me that day but when I was down at the minor tracks in the West Country, he liked to bet with me being a fellow Londoner I suppose, though I was from Islington and he was from Romford way.

Sat just in behind the leaders never more than two lengths off the pace, McCoy took it up on Liberman at the top of the hill which is a long way to go for a 25-runner flat race, so I thought to myself something's surely going to pick them up and especially when his elbows were working on the downhill run and later when he administered a smack approaching the home bend and two more rounding it.

Once into the straight the pack were coming for him but, one by one, Liberman fended them off, most latterly Trabolgan who was half a length down at the line and went on to win what were then the Sun Alliance Chase and Hennessy Cognac Gold Cup. I doubt anyone other than AP would have got him home. Seriously. He just had to get swamped but the little horse just kept sticking his game head out.

The roar of the crowd when they passed the post shook the place to its foundations. Ralphy slumped to the wooden boxes upon which

The Cheltenham Rollercoaster

Stefan shook him telling him not let the punters know we've lost, after which Ralphy stood up like a soldier on Remembrance Sunday to start paying out.

People ask me how I feel after a bad losing day but after Dettori Day nothing bothered me too much so I shrugged it off, got back to our digs, and got on with it looking at how we could get it back on the final day.

***

The Racing Post put together one of those greatest Cheltenham Festival gambles features in their build up to the meeting a few years ago which included Xenophon. Another in their list was Forgive 'N Forget who landed a right touch when he won the Coral Golden Hurdle Final in 1983 which is known as the Pertemps these days. This was also a race that also hugely affected me at the time but I am glad to report in the opposite direction.

One of the characters of the ring was the late, great Barney Curley, responsible for some spectacular betting coups, notably on Yellow Sam at Bellewstown in the seventies, the tale of which was made into a TV documentary. Then there was his four-horse betting coup that netted £2 million in 2014 which he described as "very satisfying." You are not kidding! The preparation that must have gone into pulling that off, I can't imagine. A trainee priest, he became a fearless punting hero to many and also did so much for charity setting up DAFA (Direct Aid for Africa).

Not so well known is that he owned Forgive 'N Forget in his early years before selling him to the builder Tim Kilroe but had kept his hand in the running plans for the horse who was punted into as low as 5/2 for that thirty-runner handicap hurdle at the Cheltenham Festival.

The gamble started ante-post once the weights were published after he had been given 11st 6lbs which turned out to be second-top weight but his trainer Jimmy FitzGerald thought this was the best horse he had ever had. And he was right as Forgive 'N Forget went on to win the Cheltenham Gold Cup two years later after he was controversially beaten into second in the Royal Alliance Chase a year earlier. On that occasion Johnny Francome took the 'spare' but many including *Timeform* felt that he had given him an injudicious ride from too far back.

A 19-year-old Mark Dwyer was booked to ride in the Coral Golden Hurdle Final, maybe to try and get a bigger price on the day, but as we know he went on to become a top class jockey. The race is on *YouTube* and very pleasant viewing it makes for me too as I had been having tenners on ante-post at around 10/1 whenever I could. Every time I had a winning bet then another tenner was placed so I had a stack of them stuffed in my London Red Bus money box but couldn't find out exactly how much I had riding on him until smashing it to smithereens.

It was Reggie Gibbons who had marked my card about the horse in Covent Garden flower market which was known back then as Nine Elms. He owned the wholesale business J & E Paige and had a soft spot for me. If we weren't talking about women then it was horses. He loved his racing and was one of life's good guys, a proper gent and we used to talk about racing from 5am in the morning with a double sausage and bacon sandwich.

The Cheltenham Rollercoaster

Onto the race and as cool as ice, Dwyer settles Forgive 'N Forget stone-bonking last of the thirty runners in the early stages so his connections must have filled him up with confidence before the race that this thing was a steering job. With a circuit to race he had moved up into the middle of the pack. Shortly afterwards Graham Bradley made his move on the Michael Dickinson-trained clear second-favourite Brunton Park to take it up and Dwyer took closer order at the top of the hill firmly keeping him in his sights moving into third place.

Heading down to the second-last and it was a duel between the two market leaders who had the others strewn out all across Gloucestershire but it was obvious that Forgive 'N Forget was travelling the stronger. Waiting until the final flight to take it up, he was ridden clear on the run-in to win as he liked. There was also a horse in the race that came from nowhere to run into third called, you'll never guess what? Constitution Hill!

The talk was that they landed a £1 million coup when it all added up so Barney Curley had orchestrated another monster gamble.

I was at Folkestone the day when Curley had his famous rant at John McCririck and Luke Harvey watching it unfold close up from the unsaddling enclosure so just out of shot. One of the funniest things I've ever seen and it has gone viral so well worth a watch if you haven't seen it. When I was a guest with Luke and Jason Weaver on their Friday night show on *Attheraces* I brought it up and Luke has always been fine with it.

9
Would The Real Dick Turpin Please Stand Up?

Who would have thought a barrow boy like me would be glamming it up at the likes of York, Goodwood and Ascot? I'll cover the Ascot tale later but here's a couple from York and Goodwood which, oddly enough, came only three weeks apart, and a few more for good measure, some of which I touched on in my first book.

***

I love York races. Who doesn't? Brilliant racing, brilliant facilities, brilliantly run. If only the car park was nearer for someone like me! However, July 14th 2007 will go down as a date that I want to forget.

The Knavesmire as it is often called is where they famously hanged the most infamous highwayman of them all, Dick Turpin. I wasn't around then but I do remember watching Richard O'Sullivan playing him on his trusty steed Black Bess with Swiftnick by his side, even if they romanticised it to make him out to be some kind of folk hero. He was a wrong'un.

Despite being a highwayman, the crime they actually hung him for back in 1739 was not armed robbery but, would you believe, horse theft which had been a capital offence for almost two centuries. A lot of bookies now should be called Dick Turpin the odds they offer.

FIFTY YEARS IN THE BETTING JUNGLE

This sorry tale is not so much of highway robbery but sneaky, horrible, filthy, cowardly, broad-daylight robbery and likely by someone I know.

I was working the Tote pitch at York for John Smith's Cup Day which, if you are not already aware, outside of Ebor Day is their big Saturday summer fixture. It also attracts a different kind of racegoer than for the Ebor Meeting, the prime intention for many being to get totally rat-arsed on as much of the sponsor's product that they can possibly consume. Business is therefore always very good but it can also be pandemonium. Given how tanked up many punters were, we could have bet to any price we wanted and some would keep coming back but obviously we couldn't do that for a horse racing meeting. If only it were a point-to-point back in the day!

Me, Pam Sharman and Nicky were betting on the rails but, whilst packing up, a brawl involving about 25-30 people broke out not far away behind us so we wanted to get out of there in double-quick time. I quickly grabbed the cash from out of the top of the rails stand, called a hod, which permanently stands there, and put it in a bag and headed to the car. Given how busy a day it was, it then took me the best part of two hours to get out of that car park so it was late when I arrived back home so put the bag of cash into the safe without counting it, worked out that we had a small winning day from the ledger, and settled down for a very large gin and tonic before hitting the sack.

Two days later and I was off to one of those many Windsor evenings on Mondays to meet up with Pam who had been a senior member of their on-course Tote Credit team but was now working alongside me on specific days to help man their pitch. I was showing her the

Would The Real Dick Turpin Please Stand Up?

ropes so that one day she could take over. On arrival at the Windsor betting ring, Pam asked for the float so I handed over the bag that I took home with me from York. Once she opened it, she quickly totted up that we were £10,000 short. What? How? Fuck!

The bag of cash had been kept in the safe at home and had not been touched by anyone else except me, so where was the money? And then it dawned on me. In my haste to get away from the mass fight at York, I had left £10,000 in the false bottom of the hod which only those in the game would have known about as it acted as a secret security measure. In the chaos to get out sharpish, I had left it behind.

As the betting managers, Pam and me were responsible so that was a long Monday evening at Windsor with it playing on our minds throughout. As the cash was hidden at the bottom of the hod, I thought with any luck it would still be there so at the crack of dawn the next morning I headed back up the A1 to York like Ayrton Senna and as soon as they let me through the gates I headed for the pitch.

When I opened up the secret compartment of the hod my heart sank as all that was left remaining of ten large was just a single £20 note. Someone had half-inched the rest and the same cheeky bastard had left me with a score as a thank you. I couldn't believe I had been so stupid.

It's the fact that the money was hidden in the secret compartment that makes me think it was probably someone in the game who took it. Someone who knew exactly where to look. I felt sick thinking that one of your own could have stolen it and then I phoned Pam straight away.

Feeling sorry for myself I headed off to spend the £20 on a large plate of fish and chips with mushy peas from *White's* close to the racecourse, one of the best chippies on the circuit whilst I worked out what would be my next course of action. I can't not give a shout out to *The Wetherby Whaler*, though! Different class. No cod is served there, only haddock as that is caught locally off the North Sea rather than importing from Icelandic waters. I cod you not. I digress. You want to know how I got myself out of this mess, don't you? Well, I didn't.

I went back to the racecourse and asked the security people if they had any CCTV footage but that drew a blank. That left me with no other choice but to then drive across the Pennines to the Tote's head office to see their MD Joe Scanlon in Wigan and spill the beans as to what had happened. As I knew would be the case, he said that we would have to pay it. Rather than going through all the hassle of filing a formal report and have an enquiry drag on for weeks on end I simply gave them ten grand to end it there and then.

But to whoever nicked the money, if they ever read this, I'll say to them this. Leaving that score was just adding insult to injury.

***

When the Tote bought my 67 pitches, they wanted me to run the rails to train up Pam and also part of the deal was that when she took over then my son Nicky would act as her clerk.

It was Glorious Goodwood just three weeks after the York fiasco and I was manning the Tote board on the rails minus Pam who was needed for a Newmarket Friday evening and also the following day. I love Goodwood and years ago I used to bet on Trundle Hill. The old Panama gets dusted off when I return and who doesn't like a Pimms?

The Saturday card at Goodwood's five-day jamboree is always hard as it's packed with big-field handicaps. Not only are you a hostage

Would The Real Dick Turpin Please Stand Up?

to fortune on the round course where plenty of jockeys have to ride for luck and pray that the breaks come at the right time but being on the right side of the track is a necessity for the Stewards' Cup over the straight six furlongs.

On Stewards' Cup Day I convinced Peter Jones, who was then Chairman of the Tote, to come to our pitch and join in the fun by chalking up the prices and taking the bets himself. It would be a good bit of publicity and we'd get Big Mac to cover it on *Channel 4 Racing*. Peter was a punter back in the day and wrote *The Trainers' Record* which was a punters' guide to the performance of trainers, which was basically the forerunner to all the stats we can now get our hands on daily, so he could be called somewhat of an anorak in those days and well ahead of his time.

There are three really big six furlongs handicaps; the Wokingham, Stewards' Cup and Ayr Gold Cup and they should be a bookies' benefit with such massive fields but you will be surprised over the years how well favourites have done in all of them. It's not so much about the fav though for bookies but the shorteners, though they are often one and the same.

Zidane was the 6/1 favourite for James Fanshawe and Jamie Spencer having easily won at Ascot in May but he didn't get the rub of the green when favourite for the Wokingham having to be switched a couple of times so he finished only seventh from the wrong side of the course.

Like his namesake on the football pitch, Zidane was a mercurial talent but one with his quirks as he was that type of horse that needed holding up and producing very late, so would always need luck in getting a clear run. As such he was a jolly that I wanted to take on for all we were worth, even though there was no better man than Spencer for that kind of ride.

And we did, or rather Peter did, so much so that McCririck was making the most of the story milking it for all it was worth declaring that if the favourite won then the Tote might get wiped out by its own chairman! A massive exaggeration of course but it all made for good TV which was his job with Jones declaring: "The price stays as it is - 8/1" so we got filled in.

Heading into the final furlong, the two groups had merged long beforehand so taking any potential draw bias out of it and Spencer produced Zidane to win in the very last stride by a short-head from Borderlescott who had won the race the previous year. So now Big Mac was really in his element! Watching all this unfolding at home in horror was Joe Scanlon.

Shortly after the race Peter had to leave to fulfil other commitments and left me to start paying out a big queue of happy punters which must have stretched back to Selsey Bill. Whilst paying out I got a call from Joe and he sounded most agitated. Actually, no, he was going fucking mental. The conversation started something like: "What the hell's been going on down there, how much have you done?"

Listening to Big Mac's ranting, after Zidane had won by a gnat's you know what, Joe thought that we must had done hundreds of thousands, if not more. What he didn't know was that we had backed the horse early doors so only lost £50,000. We even won on the day

Would The Real Dick Turpin Please Stand Up?

as a whole with the other results going in our favour. You couldn't buy that kind of publicity so you can add marketing genius to my list of talents!

Many years earlier whilst working at the Glorious Meeting, there was an attractive Tote girl who I was chasing. You could say that I was trying to punch above my weight in trying to snare her, but that would be hard to do! I usually stayed at the Marriott in Chichester and knew the Tote put up their staff at the Royal half an hour away in Bognor Regis.

As it was a five-day meeting and working for myself at this time, I took one of the days off to visit a women's hairdresser to dye my hair darker. To make me look more smouldering and all that to try and impress her. Yeah, I know! It happened to also be one of the hottest days of the summer. I made my way to the Royal afterwards and hit the bar hoping to see her.

Before the Tote girls headed downstairs from their rooms for the evening after a day dealing with toffs not knowing how to fill a Placepot out properly, this fella said to me: "Do you want to go to the toilet, mate?" I looked him up and down. "Not being funny" he continued, "I'd have a look at yourself in the mirror if I was you." Once I realised that I was initially getting the wrong end of the stick, I took his advice and saw the dye running down my bonce. I cleaned myself up and headed back to the bar and thanked him.

As for the Tote girl, we did meet up that evening and had a real good laugh in the bar. Oh yeah, I also ended up marrying her.

***

FIFTY YEARS IN THE BETTING JUNGLE

The tale for Epsom Downs with which I am most referenced is one that doesn't paint me in a positive light and I got some stick for it, or at least my reputation did.

No, I wasn't the infamous bogus bookmaker John Batten who in 1997 legged it from the hill which was free to the public with thousands of pounds after laying inflated prices about the Derby runners before the first race, never to be seen or heard of again!

He was offering the Even-money favourite Entrepreneur at 7/4 so even the bookies had to take some of that as it was easy for them to make a quick buck for when they opened their books. To add insult to injury to those he duped, Greg Wood in *The Independent* wrote a few days later that on his betting ticket wasn't the name of John Batten but... Lucan. You have to admire this conman's sense of humour if nothing else!

Now, you would think that amongst us on-course bookies, we might have heard a thing or two on the grapevine about his identity down the years but not a bean. He clearly was a con artist who had nothing to with the game or word would have got out.

It was Derby Day in 1989 and I was still working my way up the bookmaking ladder so was in the Lonsdale Enclosure in the middle of the course on the Downs which would have cost me about £30 a day to stand there. This was where all the day trippers turned up in their topless buses back when it was still a big day out for Londoners. Lovely, I thought, they weren't racing people and were here for a good time so working out odds percentages on each-way terms was very unlikely to be high on their list of priorities.

Would The Real Dick Turpin Please Stand Up?

Nashwan was the heavy favourite that year coming off winning the 2000 Guineas as he promised to be even better over middle distances than he was at a mile. Trained by one of the greats Major Dick Hern and ridden by another Willie Carson, after they retired both men rated him the best horse that they had trained and ridden.

Chalked up at odds-on first show in a fairly-small field for the Derby those days of just a dozen runners, and three of those started at 250/1+ with seemingly no right to be there, it was a race ripe for the each-way punter and against us layers. So, we pulled out our trump card.

I say 'we' because I was far from the only bookie who had a maximum place payout on each-way bets of 3/1 for the Derby if we had the fav priced up at odds-on, irrespective of the win odds as it was common practice those days amongst many on-course bookies, so I rolled along with it. The each-way terms were up on my board plainly for all to see so there could be no argument so it was up to punters if they wanted a piece of my action or someone else's.

The rank outsider of the field was Terimon trained by the popular Clive Brittain in the famous Beaverbrook colours. Clive had trained the brilliant filly Pebbles a few years earlier but still had a reputation for being a glass-half-full man so he wasn't afraid to run horses at very big prices in very big races. This was one such case as his grey was sent off as the 500/1 rank outsider under Mouse Roberts having needed eight races to break his maiden tag last time out at Leicester.

Now, I'm not usually one for after-timing, but as most of his runs had been over six and seven furlongs and he was bred to be a stayer by Bustino, plus this was his first try at a mile-and-a-half and coming off a win, looking back now, 500/1 did seem to be too big in a twelve-runner race. Perhaps Brittain's reputation of running supposed no-hopers in big races preceded him?

At a quarter the odds to finish in the first three, Terimon's true place odds were therefore 125/1 but I was laying only 3/1 in accordance with what was written on my board. I know, it doesn't look good and I could certainly be accused of being Dick Turpin here! That wasn't stopping the day trippers though as we were taking each-way bets on all the outsiders including Terimon, who we had at 200/1 on our board.

Nashwan actually went off at 5/4 against and won as easily as many expected but, running on five lengths into second behind him, was the stoutly-bred Terimon appreciating the greater test of stamina to finish ahead of the second-fav Cacoethes for Guy Harwood and Greville Starkey who was two lengths back in third. Nashwan went on to become the only horse to this day to add the Coral-Eclipse and King George to his 2000 Guineas and Derby victories. It was two seasons later and following good runs in other big races that Terimon finally got his day in the sun proving his Derby second to be no fluke by going on to beat the following season's Derby winner Quest For Fame into second in the 1991 Juddmonte International at 16/1.

So, it was payout time and you'll never believe it, we only got one complaint from those who collected off us having backed Terimon each-way. As for the guy who kicked up a fuss, all I did was point to the rules on my board for the Derby and then he didn't have a leg to stand on. Also, believe it or not, we actually lost on the race. Dave

Would The Real Dick Turpin Please Stand Up?

Rossi was my clerk that day who only stood in occasionally and said "We've done some here, Gal" as Nashwan proved to be very popular indeed and I kept standing him. As a bookie, if the favourite won the Derby, you lose. Simple at that.

I have to say that moving the Derby from a Wednesday to a Saturday was the worst thing they ever did. For Londoners it was a rare midweek holiday. Didn't they understand that's what made the day special? Workers had other things to do on a weekend and it also gave those people who didn't take the day off at least a chance to have half an hour break in the afternoon being Derby Day as everyone watched it back then.

***

You want a Grand National tale? Nothing too controversial here as there was only one a year so this is the best I can do.

Working in the ring for the BBC with John Parrott having taken over from Angus Loughran aka Statto off *Fantasy Football League* when covering the Grand National for the national broadcaster was one of the highlights of my career. If only my mum and dad had still been around to see their son on primetime TV for one of the biggest days in the sporting calendar.

It was 2010 so the year when McCoy won it on Don't Push It. He was a gamble in the couple of days leading up to the race having been 33/1 earlier in the week. Once it was clear that the housewives' choice AP would be riding him, he kept shortening up and did so again on the day of the race ending up as 10/1 joint-favourite following the late money from the reps to bring the price down to save on shop liabilities.

FIFTY YEARS IN THE BETTING JUNGLE

The 'Big Three' used to shorten up eight or ten horses very late on. There were 40 horses' names on those boards, so whilst the leading fancies kept shortening, the bigger-priced horses' odds largely remained the same in those final last couple of minutes.

After Don't Push It had won, many of the racing journos lambasted me and JP (that's Parrott not McManus who owned the winner!) for not reporting what his Betfair SP was as it was much higher than the SP, nearly double in fact. But I didn't want to spoil a winning bet for the TV punters. It is well known amongst clued-up punters that you have to get on early for the National and never, ever, bet SP.

***

The best day to be a bookie by a mile at Newbury was the Arab Meeting on a Sunday every August where it was free entry and they gave away big prizes to racegoers like cars and a holiday so it was jam packed.

As I had been betting on Arab Racing all over the country for 25 years at the likes of Hexham, Aintree, Huntingdon and Goodwood to name but four, I had the No.1 pitch at all of them and business was always good at Newbury. The punters weren't clued up about these horses and neither were the bookies except that we knew to keep the French runners on side as they were different gravy.

We certainly didn't know how to spell or pronounce hardly any of the names of these Arab-breds which were, how shall we put it, challenging. It also didn't help as my clerk for this day was always Deaf Jack who worked for Bobby Warren for over forty years who by the end was well into his seventies and wearing two hearing aids. So when the horse names were too long or too unpronounceable,

Would The Real Dick Turpin Please Stand Up?

sometimes we just used to chalk up the first name or the saddlecloth numbers on the board. If the Tote can do it then why couldn't we?

I used to feel for the commentator Gary Capewell but he loved the Arab Racing game and you could call him the oracle of the sport over here.

The actress Susan George used to breed, own and race Arab-breds so was a regular at this meeting and with her husband and actor Simon MacCorkindale bet with me. Sheikh Hamdan al Maktoum was present every year until his death and in a way the big Newbury day died with him.

***

I still look forward to my days manning pitches in Scotland. The first pitch I ever had on a racecourse was at Perth on the rails next to Fearless Freddie Williams. There were only two others betting on the rails; William Hill and Stan Wood who owned a post office in Fife. I really loved those days.

But there were so many bookies in Scotland betting in the ring and half of them seemed to own pubs or massage parlours. Even now their sons are still making books having taken over their pitches. Tommy Morton owned betting offices in the hard Gorbals area of Glasgow and his son Billy Morton now runs them and the racecourse pitches. He is a hard man to bet next to as Billy never lets anyone go.

One day when I was up for the Scottish Grand National, on the Thursday I rang up fellow bookie Andy Smith (aka Dick Reynolds) who owned Lil Rockerfeller twisting his arm to come up and go halves on the book. He did so but on the Friday all the favourites won so we did £54,000 between us. How he must have loved me!

FIFTY YEARS IN THE BETTING JUNGLE

We stayed at the Hilton in Glasgow so decided that night we would console ourselves by getting totally rat-arsed. On the Saturday we picked out in advance which horses we wanted to keep on side and as luck would have it they all won, so somehow we got back virtually everything. We only did £400 each over the weekend so it was like *Escape From Alacatraz* and we always laugh about it when we get together.

***

I don't bother with Kempton as it's only good for one day a year and I've never been a lover of Sandown. So, despite being a cockney, I don't know what it is about London tracks but I'd rather get in a car and drive two hours. I find it hard to win at Newmarket as most of the horses are trained there so a lot of people know what's what and it's a case of follow the money as Deep Throat said *In All The President's Men*, especially at the Craven Meeting where all the favs used to buzz in. As for their evening meetings, most of the public are there for the music and not the racing so it's quiet enough in the betting ring but loud enough with the entertainment and you need a box of Panadol.

10
The Diamond From Dagenham

I have been asked to make a book on a number of sporting events away from the norm which I didn't have the first clue about. Like when I was the first on-site bookie at Burghley Horse Trials for Totesport happily laying 100/1 about a twenty-two-year-old horse to lose around £100K which I got a dressing down for 'just in case' and Crown Green Bowls at the back of the Waterloo Hotel in Blackpool with my old pal J P Doyle (Graham Billington) for an event that has been going since 1907 and where we took serious money.

I am more than happy to open a book on any betting event for which I am not fully clued up on provided that I have exclusivity so no other competition to make it worth my while. So, when Barry Hearn requested my presence at FishOMania to take over from Harry 'The Dog' Findlay in 2005 as the lone betting operator, I jumped at the chance.

That was the first time I had any dealings with Barry so he must have chosen me as Harry's replacement as he wanted a well-known name. I'll never forget how he ended our first conversation: "I'll tell you something Gary, if you fuck me once, you'll never fuck me again." It was virtually identical the scene from *Scarface* with Tony Montana meeting the Bolivian drug lord Alejandro Sosa at his luxury mansion built into side of the stunning Andes mountain range……….but in an office in Brentwood. There's only so far that you can romanticise this tender exchange! We then shook hands and have been doing business together ever since.

For me, Harry is all and what is still great about betting. He has punted on most sports including losing £2 million on the All Blacks to win a Rugby Union World Cup. The tale of which is must reading in his autobiography but of course he has had massive betting highs too plus he was the joint-owner of the Cheltenham Gold Cup winner, Denman. The Tank, himself. But like me his first love was greyhound racing.

Barry's autobiography is also essential reading being the greatest sporting promoter of his time. It didn't matter what he asked, you just don't say no to The Diamond from Dagenham and that included when he told me at FishOMania: "Gal, take on anyone with anything they like."

A part of Barry's genius is finding sports that have previously-untapped potential and then promote them properly in his own unique way. Back in the seventies after qualifying as an accountant, he became chairman of Lucania Snooker Clubs where some beanpole ginger kid was potting balls for fun and the rest is snooker history.

Boxing, pool, golf, table tennis and ten-pin bowling also benefited from Barry's input but surely his finest hour is how he turned a pub game played by mainly ageing, sweaty, overweight, heavy drinkers, so basically me wearing a silk shirt, into the incredible success that darts is today. Once he got hold of it, he took the sport to a whole new barely-believable stratosphere.

***

The Diamond From Dagenham

Being a keen angler himself, it naturally followed that Barry turned his attentions to promoting fishing. A no-brainer really when you consider how many millions partake in the sport so he came up with the FishOMania concept which he organised to be broadcast on Sky after Greg Dyke at London Weekend Television turned him down. Thirty years later and it's still on our screens and more popular than ever. On most finals days he will arrive by helicopter to watch, relax and give out the prizes.

Having sold all my racecourse pitches to the Tote, I was still working for them as part of that deal and so it was under their banner when I chalked up my first-ever fishing book at Hayfield Lakes near Doncaster. Where on earth do I start, I thought?

There were only sixteen anglers that could take part back then which has now risen to twenty-five. There were three previous winners in the field so I put them in shorter than the rest but there was canny, local money for Marc Jones, a company director from Wakefield who was on the books for Spurs as a youngster but little did I know that he had already been backing himself in Tote offices in the week leading up to the event.

On the day I opened up at 16/1 about him but within minutes had been forced to cut him to 8/1 before he placed a lumpy bet, relatively speaking, on himself. It seemed that the whole of Yorkshire wanted a piece of the action but, as directed by Barry, I availed him every penny and then scrubbed his odds off the board for a while, later introducing him as the new 2/1 favourite. So, 16s into 2s, sound familiar? I thought, oh no here we go again!

FIFTY YEARS IN THE BETTING JUNGLE

At the half-way stage, he was already well ahead so it didn't take a bloodhound to smell that something very fishy was going on here. Turns out that he lived twenty miles down the road so the word was that he had been practicing on this lake for a while in his preparation. And there was me thinking you just slung out a rod and hoped for the best! Was I going to be hooked, lined and sinkered? It turned out to be exactly that but also gutted and placed on display at Billingsgate Market!

After Jones had won, only then was I informed that the favourite had a stronger record in this event than in the Russian Presidential Elections so these maggot drowners really knew their stuff. I took the positive approach that I was now much wiser for next year.

Turns out the only problem that Jones had was that, in time-honoured tradition, as the winner he jumped into the lake but in his celebrations he had forgotten that he still had all his betting tickets in his pocket. When he came up to collect from me, he presented this soggy, barely legible slip but he got paid and had landed himself a very nice touch. He might have had more trouble getting paid out with them in the Tote shops!

He obviously didn't fleece me for enough though as some years later he appeared on one of those *Rogue Trader* TV programmes and got sent down for three years for bullying a pensioner into releasing equity on his property. He had driven the poor man to and from the bank convincing him that he needed building work doing and paying him £36,000 for a botch job.

The Diamond From Dagenham

A few years later one of the competitors approached me to have a £50 bet on himself at 16/1. Nothing unusual in that. Steve Cooke wasn't amongst the front runners to win the prize but he had won the competition in 1999 so clearly knew his way around a tackle box. I shortened him up accordingly.

With just ten minutes before the gun fired, I get a call from the Sky Bet offices in Leeds who were betting on the event as Sky TV were covering it live. I was asked if I would take a bet off them which naturally sent some alarm bells ringing thinking that they must want to lay something off? What did they know that I didn't? Apparently, they had been inundated all week about a novelty bet at an ungenerous-looking 16/1 for any angler to catch absolutely no fish whatsoever and had taken so much cash that the odds were now down to 5/2 so asked if I would take a bet to cover some of their liabilities.

I told them that I couldn't accept it as the Tote system that I was operating wasn't set up to log that kind of bet "but if it's any consolation", so said angling expert Gary Wiltshire, "I think even I could catch at least one fish in five hours with a branch and a piece of string with a worm on a bent nail and these are career anglers so I reckon your money is safe."

He seemed relieved after my reassurance and said that he would ring back after the event had finished. Shortly after 5.30pm they already had announced the 1-2-3 so had then moved on to giving out the scores of the rest ending with Cooke in last place with "no fish." There was stunned silence.

FIFTY YEARS IN THE BETTING JUNGLE

The following day there was an official stewards' enquiry into his performance, or lack of, which The Angling Association got involved in but it came to a dead end. *The Angling Times* got in touch with me the next morning wanting to the know the story so I told them that Cooke had bet on himself with me so there seemed no case to answer so The Lord only knows what happened there?

Whilst suffering from depression in 2013, I was manning the pitch at Cudmore near Newcastle-under-Lyme so just wasn't in the right frame of mind for it.

The money came cascading in for Wirral angler Jamie Hughes so I kept shortening him up to keep my losses at a minimum but he was pulling fish out of the water like an Icelandic trawlerman and won in a hack canter hauling in an incredible 68 kilograms. I hadn't done fortunes but it wasn't about the money, I just wanted to be out of there. Like me Jamie was a fine example of a physical specimen but he's shed some timber since then and I count him as a good mate and the best in the game. He then won it again in 2015 and 2017 which is some effort as being given an unfavourable draw can kill your chances stone dead.

Another Barry 'classic' was his celebrity angling competition near Hitchin where all the proceeds went to charity including any winnings I made. I priced it up and made James Wade 4/1 favourite and offered 8/1 about Barry who then asked: "How much do I need on to make me favourite?" I said £100. He replied: "Here's one and a half and make me 3/1." The winner was Jess Harding who fought for the Heavyweight Championship of Great Britain. No one was going to argue.

The Diamond From Dagenham

Over the years I can guarantee you one thing and that's I've done my bollocks on FishOMania but I did have a right result when it returned back to Hayfield Lakes in 2018 when a 21-year-old, unfancied Brummie called Pete Black scooped the £50,000 cheque becoming the youngest winner and at 25/1 he was a complete skinner for me winning £7,800 up against experienced anglers. I didn't lay one single bet on him.

***

On the invitation of Barry Hearn, I was the on-site bookie for the Premier League Darts and one night at the Motorpoint Arena in Nottingham stands out like a sore thumb.

It was on the Thursday of the Cheltenham Festival in 2014 where we had come out around £800 to the good, which was not to be sniffed at when trying to clear a daily wage of £300-£400, so I was hoping for a good night at the darts to turn a good working day into a really good working day.

I had left Sharon in charge of the girls, Jaimee and Meghan, with some basic instructions knowing that I wouldn't be arriving until around half-way through the five games as was driving straight from Prestbury Park. As it transpired, I arrived just after the second match had finished so there were still three full games to play. Sharon was pleased to tell me that business had been brisk with the biggest bet being £20 as I had instructed with most of the other wagers being tenners and fivers. Sweet, that's the way I liked it, lots of a little as that usually meant a nice profit at the end of the night.

In the first game Peter Wright had beaten Simon Whitlock at 4/6 and then Adrian Lewis beat Gary Anderson at 4/5. Nothing too unexpected there but then, whilst sitting down to go through the many piles of betting slips, a very ugly pattern started to emerge. At least three-quarters of the bets were accumulators on the five favourites and the three best players in the world of Phil Taylor, Michael van Gerwen and Raymond van Barneveld had yet to play! I thought, we're in big trouble here.

All gamblers know the power of an accumulator, it can hit a bookie for six, no matter how short the prices involved are. I quickly worked out that if the last three favourites all won then it would pay out about 12/1 so all those many Scores, Cock and Hens and Lady Godivas were seriously adding up and looking much bigger bets now. This was getting serious and I started to feel sick as I sloped off to the back of the arena to watch the torture unfold. And darts is pure torture for punters as no other sport puts you through the wringer more than if you have had a bet with so many ups and downs in one match. Set play is even worse but at least this was a race to seven legs.

The third game on was Michael van Gerwen versus Wes Newton for which the Dutch superstar was a heavy favourite but Wes was capable of beating anyone on his day. It had already been a very long day so I was totally bolloxed and falling asleep even in the face of a big payout during that game in which Mighty Mike went on to trounce Newton 7-1. My mood wasn't lifted when I heard that Newton had averaged 103 so he just met MVG on one of his very best nights. Had Wes been up against anyone else that night he likely would have won.

That left me with two games to save my shirt: Raymond van Barneveld vs Robert Thornton followed by Phil Taylor versus Dave Chisnall and no one could see The Power not winning the finale so

The Diamond From Dagenham

I was pinning all my hopes on The Thorn. Staring at a loss of about eleven grand and only having 6K on me as I was not expecting to need anything like that amount, in fact it was all I had, there were going to be lots of very disgruntled, beered-up Billy Bunters queuing up for their winnings that couldn't get paid out on the same night which was not a prospect that I was relishing. In fact, I was bricking it but couldn't let on in front of the girls.

In my desperation I tried to get hold of Barry to explain the predicament I had found myself in but failed. So then I got onto his right-hand man Matt Porter who was on the premises and nothing is too much trouble for him. He told me that by a stroke of luck the locally-based World Super Middleweight Champion Carl Froch was a guest of his for a night out so if Barney beat Thornton, then he would send him down to our pitch just in case there was any trouble. The Cobra himself, lovely.

That took some pressure off but Matt also said not to worry because, if necessary, he would collect all the bar takings so by hook or by crook everyone would get paid on the night. So at least we had a Plan B and I'd worry about my personal losses later if it came to that, which looked short odds.

Barney won the opening two legs. Do I head for the doors now, I thought, only for Thornton to level it up. After nine legs the Scot had gone into a 5-4 lead so he just needed one more leg to ensure a tie at worst to get me out of this mess as thank God we weren't betting 'Draw No Bet' so a 6-6 draw would have been enough to knock out all the fivefold accas. Two legs later however and Barney was now 6-5 up with just one leg to play so I was counting, make that praying, on

Thornton taking advantage of 'having the darts' in the final leg so he was to throw first.

He started with a maximum. One hunnnnnnnundred and eighty thundered Russ Bray in his own inimitable style. It was the sweetest sound that I had heard all night so exhaled a big blow from my cheeks as that felt like half the job done 'with the darts'. Up stepped Barney. Just a ton. Thornton moved to the oche again and I looked away. Thud, thud, thud. One hunnnnnnnundred and eighty! So by now he was miles clear. Up stepped Barney again. Another ton. Not enough. Thornton's next three arrows going for a nine-darter to tie the match were a bag of spanners but he had left a two-dart finish of 81. Barney steps up again. One hunnnnnnnundred and eighty! You have got to be kidding me!

So now up stepped The Thorn to close it out. Most pros would go treble nineteen and then double twelve. In looped the first dart straight into the centre of that red treble segment only for the second dart to land high of the double twelve and the third arrow inside the wire leaving double six. I couldn't take the pressure so looked away again as Barney had 121 for the match.

The cheers from the crowd told me that he hit the treble nineteen with his first dart leaving sixty-four which meant treble sixteen to leave double eight but thankfully he missed that next treble but had set it up to leave double sixteen and everyone knew that Barney wouldn't miss again with three darts in hand.

Thornton had been given a second chance and it was now or never. It had only been a few months since coming through depression and if this result went the wrong way it might have pushed me right back

The Diamond From Dagenham

in the wrong direction as the six grand in my pocket was all that I had in the world at the time and then I'd have to find another five on top of that.

I couldn't watch again so waited for the crowd reaction to tell me everything. *Ooooh*. Thornton had obviously missed with the first dart. Then an even louder *ooooh* a couple of seconds later. This was unbearable. And finally, the huge cheer that I yearned to hear so badly and, just like that, those 11K losses had turned into a tidy profit. That's the difference a millimetre can make. Sport and punting can all be about the finest of margins. But the relief I felt there and then, I can't put it into words and it turned out that Robert was a thorn in the punters' side that night and not mine.

Matt Porter made his way down after the game: "Never in doubt" he beamed. He started out as the office junior and now runs the PDC with Adam Perfect, who I go a long way back with, as his No. 2 who as it turned out couldn't have been a more perfect choice. Proper People.

Taylor then beat Chizzy in the final game 7-5 so that too went down to the final leg so can you imagine what that would have done to my ticker on top of the previous game if Match Four hadn't gone our way? It possibly would have broken me. But it was over and the next day I went back to the Friday of the Cheltenham Festival and won well there so, for anyone just looking at that week's ledger, we had a good week. Little would they have known, and just like on a golf score card, it doesn't matter how but how many.

Believe it or not virtually the same thing happened again in Aberdeen a few years later when I was at Chelmsford instead so I sent Lofty and Sharon, who was in wheelchair with a broken foot, up north by plane and my instructions were don't get involved, meaning no big bets.

However, although they refused any big bets as instructed, the same mistake was made again in accepting far too many accas on the five favourites. On this occasion the first four jollies had won so now it was all down to Match Five between Michael van Gerwen, who was out on his own as the clear best in the world at the time back then, and Big John Henderson who would have been ranked in the thirties, maybe higher, so what chance did we have of another Scot saving our skins against a Dutchman all over again? MVG would have been about 2/9 to win the game.

Now Hendo wouldn't normally be good enough to play in the Premier League but for this particular year the PDC had introduced a concept called 'The Challenger' whereby a local player to that week's venue was invited to get a taste of the action. Being held in Aberdeen, The Highlander from nearby Huntly got the call up so he was going to have the whole arena on his side, bar those waiting for MVG to win for the accas of course and I bet they kept quiet!

Had I been there, I would have ensured that we had stopped taking accumulators after a while and these days I now only take a maximum of trebles on any slip…..under doctor's orders!

Leaving Chelmsford, I noticed a load of missed calls which all came in at once so there must have been signal issues. I thought what's happened here, was the flight delayed or had they just missed it? So, it was only after all the matches had finished that I knew any part of

The Diamond From Dagenham

the story and, praise The Lord, it was a miracle! The man with what can only be described as the most ridiculous throwing action that you have seen in your life had just managed to get a 6-6 draw against the unstoppable Green Machine.

How Sharon and Lofty would have paid out on the night had MVG won I don't know but, one thing is for certain, the partisan home crowd who were revved up even more after Big John's walk-on included a fully-kitted out piper on the bagpipes like a scene out of *Braveheart*, had helped lift their son to a higher level. Van Gerwen is a truly great player but he's only human and he really doesn't like it when the crowd gets on his back so they more than played their part in saving us thousands.

The following year I saw John in a bar at another event so, after telling him the story of how he got me out of a very deep hole, we made sure I got a photo with me waving a large wedge of notes in the air cuddling up next to him, Loadsamoney-style for those old enough to remember Harry Enfield.

When the darts venue is a good distance away then Barry puts me up in the same hotel as the players so I've got to know a few of them down the years. I owe him a lot, he's a man of the people and proper grafter. Funnily enough, I get on best with Michael van Gerwen who calls us 'The Bookie Family' but I've not told him that story!

Every year Barry invited me and the family to the PDC Darts Awards when it was going and it was a great night celebrating the previous year. We were only a small cog in the Matchroom machine where everyone is in evening dress but Barry never forgets you.

FIFTY YEARS IN THE BETTING JUNGLE

One of my regular punters at the darts nights up north killed The Yorkshire Ripper in 2020. Straight up! Not on purpose of course but after hearing his story I'd price it up as a 5s ON shot. See what you think?

After three decades at Broadmoor Hospital for the mentally insane as some would call it, having being diagnosed with paranoid schizophrenia, Peter Sutcliffe was transferred to HMP Frankland Prison in County Durham in 2016 where he had heart problems, or lack of heart problems more like it, which is where my darts-punting client, who is a decent arrowsmith himself, worked as a prison officer. Four years later and after feeling dizzy, Sutcliffe was transported to hospital to have a pacemaker fitted and it was this budding Bobby George, who doesn't shut up by the way so the Ripper would have had his ears chewed off, was given the job of being chained to him throughout the day including transportation and then bedside at the hospital.

After an extended shift of twenty hours as they had to wait on the arrival of a secure ambulance, my darts punter finally returned home in the wee hours having started to feel off colour as early as during the handcuffing arrangements. The following morning this had progressed to a full-blown cough so he tested himself for Covid and it came up positive. Just a few days later Sutcliffe was declared dead having contracted the virus but the darts man still lives on! So, at 1/5 would you be a layer or a player?

Before the PDC evolved under Barry, darts was run by the BDO and Olly Croft when Eric Bristow, Jocky Wilson and John Lowe were the three biggest names in the game. At this time the World

The Diamond From Dagenham

Championship was covered by the BBC where the King of the Lakeside, Bob Potter, who died last year at the grand old age of ninety-four and claimed that he was the inspiration for Peter Kay's Brian Potter in *Phoenix Nights*, ran a thriving club.

He liked his coin so made security search for food and drink on everyone entering the club including even those who worked there so they took away the food that we brought along for the day. We used to bring our own grub and travel up and down from Nottingham daily to keep the expenses down.

When Coral pulled out of betting there on-site, I was asked by Bob if I wanted to stand a pitch and didn't need a second invitation after agreeing that we would pay a grand for the rent for exclusivity which we did for five years straight. Despite punters needing to be on *The Krypton Factor* to find where they stuck us near the merchandise stand, which wasn't even in the auditorium, it was still a busy week and the first time we pulled into the car park we were amazed at how many coaches there were.

Tuesdays were always especially busy for me as every year the travelling community from the Aldershot area came for that particular night and they really liked a bet. Two best mates always bet with me. In one match one had a monkey on at 4/5 on Player A and the other did the same at 4/5 on Player B. Why they didn't have the bet between themselves I don't know!

It was a great atmosphere and great days. I only bet on events that I enjoy but have yet to be asked to make a book on Miss Universe.

***

FIFTY YEARS IN THE BETTING JUNGLE

Barry, of course, went on to become the chairman of Leyton Orient, stepping in to secure the club's future when they were bang in trouble. Watch the documentary called *Club For A Fiver*. It's a belter.

One Saturday they were playing at home in the FA Cup and he wanted me to set up a pitch to take bets. I can't remember the scoreline but it was something ridiculous so we cleaned up on the correct score market. However, we didn't bother again as being pitched up behind the Orient end, the liabilities on a home win were horrendous as all the outright market bets were one-way traffic, so we didn't risk that again. We got away with it that time.

Another one-and-gone experience was for a night at the boxing and a Tony Bellew fight in his home town of Liverpool. On a card featuring 1/33 shots all night long apart from the championship fight, I wasn't even getting close to getting my plums tickled apart from in which round there would be knockout and, of course, the locals only wanted to be on the hometown boy in the title bout. I just didn't like the whole experience to be honest with you but one thing I remember well was that Arg from *The Only Way Is Essex* wouldn't leave me alone all night! I'm such an A-List name dropper.

Clay Pigeon Shooting. That was another one Barry set up for me. "Where are you going next weekend, Gary?" I replied that I had no plans. "Yes, you have, you're going to Gloucestershire." It's fair to say those present and I came from very differing backgrounds.

This one fella opened up the back of his range rover, pulled out eight grand and said he wanted to avail himself of the 8/1 I was offering about him. But he wanted it each-way to which I informed him that there was more chance of me swimming The English Channel. I laid

The Diamond From Dagenham

him a grand to win eight only for Barry to tell me to let him have the lot on. This would be the only time that I went against him as the return was too strong. He finished second and we won about £2,000 all told that day. However, it was the hardest two grand that I ever won as all I heard all afternoon was bang, bang, bang, bang, bang, bang.

I have been the on-site bookie at both the Crucible Theatre and Ally Pally for the World Snooker Championship and Masters and also the three-day Shoot Out when it was held in Blackpool in December. One year we arrived early on the Friday and it was Baltic so we spent the afternoon in a William Hill in Fleetwood. That didn't go too well as the three grand float that I arrived with for the pitch was down to £300 by the time the evening games started so we needed a good first night.

The thing about the Shoot Out, every game is just ten minutes so it was very busy with a regular flow of punters with 32 matches a day. So busy, that by the end of the three days we had got all of it back having done our absolutes before it even started.

These games are basically a coin flip but punters generally still wanted to be with the bigger name who was usually favourite. I do know one punter who wins on this event betting on it in the auditorium. Courtsiding some would call it when you get a split-second edge over the TV punter. No player wants to break off these days leaving their opponent with a chance of being 'first in' for such a short format so when he sees who won the lag, he then very quickly gets on the other player on the exchange.

I had a mate who was courtsiding at the Las Vegas Desert Classic darts which ended in 2009. On one of the three days' play he would be trying to conceal himself from security on the phone to a pal back in the UK telling him what was going on a few seconds before the satellite signal had caught up. They ended up winning just over a grand which paid for his trip which was the whole point but he wasn't so cock-a-hoop when he found out that he had done his nuts on the data roaming charges when he got his phone bill!

***

During some of my hardest times Barry stood by me and he has always been there for me and deserves all the success and accolades that he has had in his life especially his OBE. This includes in horseracing as with his wife Susan they own Mascalls Stud and, amongst other Group race winners, they bred the Ascot Gold Cup hero Subjectivist trained by Mark Johnston. Just think what he could have done with British racing if he got his hands on it. He's a winner. He's a diamond. The Diamond of Dagenham.

11
The Towcester Files

As Towcester had been my local course for many years, I always wanted to own a horse to win there. Unfortunately, I never realised that dream.

David Wintle always told me you don't want to lay one out for a touch at Towcester as that hill can beat any horse. So, we didn't try. This was confirmed to me when the chief exec Kevin Ackerman told me that he was having a chat with Paul Nicholls at an awards bash and asked him why he didn't have any runners at the course and was told pointedly: "Because it fucks them."

So Towcester didn't attract many good horses. It did once host a Champion Hurdle Trial which featured Collier Bay v Relkeel v Escartefigue but, apart from that, quality horses to attempt that unforgiving hill were few and far between. Before he became a really good horse though, Marlborough was supposed to run there but, somehow, he manged to escape the racecourse and ended up running loose down the A5.

Not only did I get involved with gg.com who were based at Lord Hesketh's wing of his stately home on the other side of the back straight but also the greyhound track when that opened and I appeared on a good few Cheltenham Preview panels there.

FIFTY YEARS IN THE BETTING JUNGLE

One of the best days I ever had at any racecourse was when AP McCoy rode his 4000th winner at Towcester. J P McManus was present to watch his man hit that landmark and when he did he then bought everyone on the racecourse a drink which must have been some bar tab with over 4,500 present to see the feat. What a man.

So it was a very sad day when the stiffest course in the country closed for horseracing in 2018. You must think that any course which I touch that I hold any affection for closes down! Not so much the Midas Touch but the Deadly Touch. Think Uncle Albert off *Only Fools And Horses* and boats. That was me and greyhound tracks and racecourses!

The greyhound track also closed at the same time but only for just over a year and I'm pleased to say that it is back and still hosts the Greyhound Derby which will have its 100th anniversary in two years so I hope that everyone involved in the game goes to town to mark he occasion.

***

I think it was during Robert Bellamy's tenure as clerk when *Top Gear* recorded a segment of the show during the racing. After I had taken our bets, Jeremy Clarkson was driving a Citroen on the inside of the course on that rough piece of track with large pot holes and stones whilst they filmed the race wanting to recreate how the BBC used to cover the Grand National in the 1970s to show off the car's famed suspension and how steady they could hold the camera.

On this particular day it had chucked it down so conditions were filthy on and off the track. Clarkson was therefore told to

The Towcester Files

drive slightly behind the leaders. Once the flag was raised, being a boy racer he was a bit keen on the old accelerator and got off to a flying start so found himself a few lengths in front of the field. Still leading down the back straight on the second circuit, Clarkson then hits this giant area of standing mucky water and slop, splashing its contents all over the horses and jockeys who came back into the weighing room looking like Andy Dufresne after he escaped prison in *The Shawshank Redemption*.

Unfortunately for Jezza, the worst affected horse only happened to be trained by Ginger McCain who went fucking berserk afterwards. It took him an age to calm him down from his incandescent rage including threatening to deck Clarkson but Ackerman intervened by giving him a bottle of single malt from the well-stocked Hesketh Family cellar which soon placated him.

***

I enjoyed many great years betting on course at Towcester as business was good being well attended due to their free-entry policy with a good atmosphere which led to a vibrant betting ring.

Back in December 2003 a group of the on-course books had an early Christmas present as in the first race at Towcester there was a 1/5 ON favourite trained by Alan King so we hatched a plan. Please don't be naive in thinking this kind of thing was a one-off, it was a practice that on-course bookies had been up to since legalised betting shops came into the high streets in 1961.

A few of us chatted early doors and decided that we would have a few quid each-way against the long-odds-on favourite with something and landed on Cetti's Warbler for which the morning tissue was 14/1.

FIFTY YEARS IN THE BETTING JUNGLE

Therefore, we contrived to get its odds knocked out to 100/1 so we were getting 20/1 for our place money in the shops if he could finish in the first three. As such we made sure the favourite hardened up and he was returned at 2/17.

John Pegley was known as 'The King of the Knockout' and he was the ringleader behind the operation being notorious for pushing prices out to back them at SP.

I was not at Towcester that day but my son was manning my pitch. I was in Pontypridd attending the funeral of the Welsh bookmaker John Harris but we managed to find a few betting shops on route having £50 each-way on Renee Robeson's grey mare at starting price. After the service had finished, I found the local William Hill in the High Street and looked up at the screen. I couldn't believe my eyes when I saw it had not only just gone and won but also that the SP was 100/1 that we were looking to push it out to!

Well, you could hear the squeals of the off-course bookies who we had hit as none of the firms were happy but they paid, eventually. However, only after withholding payment for seven-to-fourteen days after a BOLA enquiry. They knew it was a crooked move but couldn't prove anything. Where was Wiltshire they asked? He had to be involved. At a funeral in the Valleys! So NOT GUILTY YOUR HONOUR. I wasn't expecting any problems collecting when we placed the bets as I wasn't expecting it to win. We were all happy in advance to be picking up a grand per ticket if the horse placed which was the hope but alarm bells went off when the firms realised that there were an abnormal number of 100/1 winning slips returning £6,000. That Christmas we had two turkeys and six Christmas puds.

The Towcester Files

A nice postscript to this story was that David Ashworth of *The Racing Post* was doing his annual pre-christmas challenge of trying to win a grand for charity and he only went and backed Cetti's Warbler. So there he was on the front page of the trade rag the next day waving his arms in jubilation.

***

When gg.com started, being based close to the racecourse I was asked if I would provide a column looking back at the action from the betting ring over the previous week from tracks where I had been. John Stubbs had been doing this in his Ringlets column for *The Sporting Life* many years before and Simon Nott is the current-day equivalent for a Star Sports column.

They eventually sold on the domain name for millions to a Chinese children's website and were rebranded gg.co.uk but my involvement ended well before then.

During that time, I appeared on some of Towcester's Cheltenham Preview Evening panels which were always great fun. Paddy Brennan was on the panel with me for 2010, a very good year for him as it turned out, as well as Mark 'The Couch' Winstanley with Robert Cooper as the genial presenter. I can't remember who else was supposed to be there but, anyway, they pulled a sickie. It must have been someone else with a 'reputation' as with a panel like that I know they were tempted to market it as the XXX-Rated Cheltenham Preview night but in the end thought better of it, especially as someone far more sensible in good judge Andrew Mount was also advertised to be on the panel.

Knowing that we were a man down at the preview night, a plan was concocted to get a well-informed and highly-opinionated local lad up on stage to add even more spice to an already outspoken panel. So, at the beginning Sir Bob was instructed to ask anyone in the audience if they wanted to take the vacant seat to raise their hand. About half a dozen did and Gavin The Hangman was chosen, as pre-planned. All the panel were in on this.

The evening progressed with the usual 'this is a certainty' and 'this can't win if it started now' bluster as everyone's opinion on these panels gets multiplied ten times over. The Hangman wasn't keen on virtually every horse set to run at the whole meeting and wasn't backward in coming forward with his opinions which he put across very bluntly.

And throughout the night he kept calling horses that he was especially in contempt of as being "rotting corpses" to the extent that I had to ask him if he was an undertaker!? One of the referred to "rotting corpses" was the novice Pigeon Island who was winless in seven chases and who Paddy was going to ride in the Grand Annual but even his presence on the panel was clearly not going to stop The Hangman from laying into the horse which led to a very lively exchange between the pair.

Paddy being Paddy, for starters he was not going to let that go without slamming him down but at the same time I doubt that he was ever going to say "this is the day, lads" but he wasn't putting anyone off the horse at the same time so I took the hint. Riding on a wave of confidence after just winning the Gold Cup on Imperial Commander, Paddy gave the battle-hardened grey in the Mould colours a peach to come from virtually last to first to win at 16/1. He even referenced the spat when being interviewed on the horse's back

The Towcester Files

waiting to be greeted by the crowd, though in more genteel terms getting his own back "some people doubted this horse" in a direct swipe at The Hangman.

Ironic therefore when Paddy got exactly the same treatment from Nico de Boinville when he was walking back to the winners' enclosure on Constitution Hill having been anti his chances of even lining up for the Christmas Hurdle, let alone winning. One thing I will say about Paddy, of all the Cheltenham panels I have been on, I'd say he was the most astute analyst of the jockeys. So now that he's not riding so not trying to appease potential owners and trainers anymore, I am looking forward to hearing him let rip.

***

In 2014, the Towcester owner Lord Hesketh and Kevin Ackerman got in touch to sound me out on developing a greyhound track in the middle of the course that they were already constructing, so we met up at the Dorchester on Park Lane in Mayfair and had five bottles of the finest Chablis for lunch. The closest I had got to that establishment before was charging the rent on the monopoly board.

It's fair to say that Lordy, as he affectionally known to his friends, enjoys the finer things in life, you know like having your own Formula 1 racing team in the 1970s, that kind of thing. Hesketh Racing was unusual as they refused any sponsorship and also gave James Hunt his big break as depicted in the film *Rush*. Silverstone is just down the road from his Easton Neston Estate which includes the racecourse. He was also a Conservative peer in the House of Lords where he was Maggie Thatcher's chief whip and treasurer of the party during the early part of the century before switching his allegiance to UKIP some years later. She and Denis enjoyed a day at Towcester races more than once when staying as his overnight guests.

They showed me their plans for what would be Britain's newest and best greyhound track and they were out of this world. For an industry dying on its arse this was a chance to resuscitate a sport on life support. I told them they couldn't fail and then they asked if I wanted a pitch on site? I didn't need asking twice so bit their hand off only for BAGS to put the kybosh on it on opening Gala Night. They vetoed my presence for reasons I highlighted earlier.

Ackerman stood up on my behalf and they agreed to meet half-way in that my pitch could be present but that there was no way I could be manning it. As such I arranged for Sharon and Nicky to stand up front whilst I would be sat in the car corresponding by walkie-talkie. I still had to be present as I was the licence holder. You just couldn't make it up. It wasn't the same as being the man up front and although we won on the first night.

In the next six weeks without me overlooking it properly when only the faces turned up, which included a huge gamble by Terry Dartnell and his owners, we did our bollocks so I had to knock it on the head.

12

Characters From The Betting Jungle

In my fifty years in the betting jungle, I have come across so many incredible people from both sides of the fence.

Good people, bad people, clever people, not so clever people, so I want to namecheck a good few that I have not already mentioned earlier. It could have been many more, believe me, so this is my little trip back down memory lane to the days when the main reason people came to the races was to hand cash over and have a bet. Remember those times?

Some of the bookies, punters and tic-tacs I reference sound like they could have come from straight out of a Guy Ritchie film.

***

The Punters.

Let's start with Jesus, shall we? Bearded John Noakes so not the one from *Blue Peter*. A big gambler but he vanished from the scene when the betting exchanges arrived. A good punter who I took on and paid the price so was well pleased to see the back of him.

Dodger McCartney was a legendary punter. He knew everyone in the game and it was a tragic day when he died in a car accident on his way back from Worcester races having just recovered from throat cancer. I attended his funeral which was jam-packed with bookies, punters, trainers and jockeys and the eulogy was given by Grand National-winning trainer, Nick Gaselee. Simon was called 'Dodger' for his uncanny knack of slipping through big crowds in the ring to get his bets on. He never bet odds-on, preferring two win-only singles in a race instead. He was a hard man to beat.

Very sadly we lost Johnny Lights last year. He was a fearless punter-turned-bookie who appeared on one of Simon Nott's Star Sports 'Racing People' interviews on *YouTube* not long before the end, so you can watch him talking about his life from both sides of the betting ring whilst laying down in his hospital bed. So named as his father owned a fruit market stall with lights all over it, therefore the name got passed down to him. He always said that he wasn't a good judge of horses but a good judge of judges and tells the story of how he used to follow Barney Curley round the ring. I used to go on holiday with him sometimes so he is sadly missed. A great family man.

One of my favourite Johnny Lights stories was at Leicester when they used to hold a hunters' chase day. On this one occasion it was hammering it down so with three races still to run he told me that he was off early to catch a show in London with his wife, Megan. To pay for the night he told me to back the fav at SP in the last for him to win £400. The tissue was 4/9 ON but by the last race in the sodden conditions the bookies had mostly disappeared leaving just me and two others. We decided we'd all open up at 1/4 ON thinking that no one would touch it at those odds, take a few quid on the other two that we didn't fancy, and then lengthen the favourite back out. Then The Undertaker suddenly appeared!

Characters From The Betting Jungle

He was usually an odds-on dog punter and steamed in with £800 to win two with all three of us so we all cut it to 1/6 ON. This meant that I now had to have £2,400 on so that Johnny could pay for his West End show night out. So, it to all intents and purposes it was a cert. Anyway, somehow it contrived to get itself rolled over.

Wanting to give him the rub up I asked him the next morning: "How was the show, John? What did you go and see?" He didn't hold back. "Fuck the fucking show! How the fuck did you get that fucking horse to start at fucking six to fucking one on!?" It was classic Lights!

Lights was the best entertainment that you could have on a night out. To cheer me up on the Saturday after Dettori Day he took me to David Martin's party. He was the top ticket agent in London and we ended up in a theatre on the south bank. It was a great night until the master of ceremonies then started reading out messages and asked the audience: "Is there a Gary Wiltshire in the house?" I stood up to make myself seen, which wasn't difficult, and then he asked: "I've just received a message from Frankie Dettori and he's asked, how's your week been, Gary!?" Just what I needed! But that was Lights' warped sense of humour.

Taking fearless to a different level was Harry 'The Dog' Findlay with his sidekick, Glen Gill. Dogs were Harry's main thing and he re-opened up Brandon near Coventry in 2012 and gave it a real good go for three years, so when it closed again that would have hit him. A great judge of all sports, I attended a few golf and snooker tournaments with him.

FIFTY YEARS IN THE BETTING JUNGLE

Henry and Joyce Gould owned a woodyard opposite Drayton Manor Park. Henry's bet was always the same - £6,000 on the returned favourite. Sometimes he would call up my betting shop with that same bet. On one occasion when he did just this, there was a 2/7 favourite in the first at Ponty that he wanted to be with so the bet was struck only for the horse to be withdrawn at the start leaving him on the inherited 7/2 fav who got beat. Upset by this, he went 'on the chase' so kept having the same bet throughout the whole card and they all got beaten too. Win, lose or draw, Henry insisted on settling up at the following meeting and, anyone who didn't, then he'd never play with them again.

Alan Potts was a proper old-school punter and still is. We always have a chat when we are at the same course together, mainly Salisbury, and he is just an all-round good bloke. Best known for writing *Against The Crowd* back in the mid-nineties, he was another hard man to beat having taken horse watching to another level, especially how they strode out on their way to post. I was standing on the rails for the Tote at Newmarket one Friday evening when the Hills rep backed a 10/1 shot with me called Forest Fire of Ben Hanbury's. I asked him why and he told me that Potts had backed it at 12s with their team on course at Newbury in the afternoon. So I sent my lad round backing it. He won and was returned at 7/1 following solid course support. Alan is now a noted expert on French racing.

Sticking with authors and in his autobiography, *A Bloody Good Winner*, Dave Nevison recounts the story that he had arranged for someone to be at the course to buy a horse out of a claimer on his behalf and how he got a phone call that evening asking if it was him

Characters From The Betting Jungle

because, if it was, the previous owners wanted it to be let known in no uncertain terms that "they are not happy." Dave wasn't for turning and informed the caller that he would take any more threats direct to the police, only to be told that he was just the messenger boy but these were "very serious people" and he would have no option but to give them Dave's phone number. Nev replied: "Give them my number, I don't care." Sure enough his phone rang again ten minutes later but this time it was another voice and the new caller made it as clear as he could that they wanted their horse back. Not only did they want the horse back, they wanted £2,000 on top for the inconvenience.

After making a few enquiries Nev then finds out the true identity of the previous owners and he goes on to say in his book that he rang a bookmaker who he thought might know them. Well, that bookmaker turned out to be me. After hearing what he had to say, without any hesitation I told him: "You better give it back and you know what, Dave, that might just be the best two grand you ever spent." So, when you see him now in the *Racing TV* studio with his *Lovejoy* hair do, spare a thought that he's still with us! Dave was a hard man to beat on the all-weather tracks.

There was one guy many years ago at the London dog tracks, mainly the Stow and Hackney, called One Armed Lou. You will never guess why. He knew the local scene inside out and attended all the trials so a Lady Godiva bet from him on an outsider was a tip in itself. You could take his bet and lay it off and chalk the dog up a few points shorter and he wasn't often wrong. He took bets himself on the amateur Sunday football at the *Hare and Hounds* in Leyton.

FIFTY YEARS IN THE BETTING JUNGLE

The QPR and England footballer Stan Bowles used to be a regular at the London dog tracks in the late-seventies. One time at Wimbledon he was alongside his team mate Don Shanks who had a gorgeous blonde on his arm. I thought, hello, he's punching above his weight. Turns out it was Miss World! Mary Stavin was her name from Sweden and she went on to be a Bond Girl in a couple of films. Bowles was a one off, one of the true mavericks of the game but a maniacal gambler. He had a reputation for drinking, womanising and gambling but, just like with George Best, when he ran onto a football pitch none of that affected his talents. The word was that he was seen putting on bets only half an hour before home kick-offs at the bookies across the road and during the match would be asking fans if he had won?

Another punter back in the day resembled Roger de Courcey, minus Nookie the Bear I am pleased to say. He purposely would always leave it very late and then come at you waving a wad of notes just as the last horse was entering the stalls. I never knocked him back as I knew Adam Pettit was a losing punter. Sure, he had some winners but even Tottenham win now and again. These days we are trained to look out for problem gamblers. He'll love that! For example, if the same punter has had a few losing biggish bets with you, we have to ask them are you in control? The usual reply to me is "fuck off you fat bastard." Adam's dream is for his boy to play for Spurs and he's going the right way so watch out for the name.

Charlie Eden was a Brummie legend who was even worse for leaving it as late as possible as he used to wait until they were Under Orders as loved getting the satisfaction about not leaving the bookie enough time to run around to try to lay some of it off.

Characters From The Betting Jungle

Two of the big names at Coolmore were faces in the ring back in the day. Derrick Smith was a rep for Ladbrokes and of course Michael Tabor was a former bookie having owned Arthur Prince. Where would racing be today without these big owners?

One day at Leicester when Michael was punting, I played him for five races and was nicely up. In the last race though, there were just four runners and he owned one of them trained by Neville Callaghan and I thought to myself, hmmm, I'm not sure I fancy laying this one too much! He hadn't flown in by helicopter for nothing. Therefore I upped sticks and left early. So the next time our paths crossed he gave it to me both barrels at how I never gave him the chance to win it back. I took it on the chin as knew that he was right.

The Ladbrokes owner Cyril Stein used to bet with me when having a day off at the races and I laid him any stakes up to five grand. If he won, he drew the readies but, if he lost, then I had to send the invoice to Rayners Lane. He was the first to employ reps to shorten up horses. Like Tabor he was from the East End. The son of 'Honest Jack' who worked at the agency that relayed info between the off-course bookmakers and racecourses, he bought Ladbrokes in the mid-1950s when it was a modest enterprise and turned it into a multibillion-pound leisure conglomerate. An Orthodox Jew, he was never at the track on Saturdays being the Jewish Sabbath and eventually settled in Israel. One of bookmaking's greats.

Alan Argiband was a face on the West-Country circuit and nine times out of ten when you saw Al, you saw H (Harry Redknapp) with him. He had very good contacts so when he backed something with me, I then backed it myself. I also used to see him in a Coral shop in Southbourne when I was staying down with my sister Jackie. Her husband Richard Cooke used to play for Spurs and Harry signed him when he was manager at Bournemouth.

I miss not seeing Steve Lewis Hamilton at the racecourse but like so many faces when the exchanges took off, they just disappeared. He went on to have his own advisory service and his big story on the Cheltenham Preview night circuit when Istabraq kept winning the Champion Hurdle was that he was the underbidder.

The Couch was some sight to behold on the racecourse and could be seen in the paddock at Cheltenham hob knobbing with the landed gentry in their finest country wear sporting his bright blue shell suit. He just didn't care. On the subject of tracksuits, of course there was Tracksuit Dave who was another Dodger McCartney as everyone knew him on the southern scene.

Martin Pipe's right-hand man was the former English table tennis champion Chester Barnes who ran the Pipeline tipping service. When we were at Pontins, he used to do exhibitions and was taking on allcomers with a frying pan. When he appeared in the betting rings wanting to back something from Nicholashayne, you ran for cover.

When The Three Musketeers from Sheffield wanted to play you also had to be on your guard. Nigel Troth, Dave Kaye and Billy the Putter-oner were very clever. They won on the horses but the dogs was their real speciality.

Scotch Paul was a big face over the border. He used to work for The Magic Sign and was one of the shrewdest betting shop punters. Not many of them win and he's been barred from more bookmakers than I've had hot dinners.

Characters From The Betting Jungle

Billy Foulkes, Bob The Dog and The Jellied Eel Man were handy punters to know. Billy always had a bag of jewellery with him so if you wanted a gold chain or ring, he was your man. When he won, he was a good winner but when he lost, he was a terrible loser. Bob the Dog was from the West End of London and arrived at racecourses with a load of stolen ties which he sold mainly to bookies. He was a horrible creature. The Jellied Eel Man used to flog them out of the boot of his car at Worcester, Stratford and Towcester so I always looked forward to attending those tracks.

Then there was Novice Hurdle Mick who would only play on horses priced up between 1/2 and 1/10 in novice hurdles so he didn't hang around too often after the first race. Another who specialised in odds-on betting was Jerry White from Ramsgate who travelled everywhere by train so when he turned up you knew you were going to be laying a favourite.

Kevin Casey was not only a bookie for Arab racing and point-to-points but he was also UK's top paddock judge, but not for racing! He was close pals with the amateur rider Angel Jacobs who had come over from America and claimed that he was the godson of Angel Cordero but he was banned for failing a drug test out there in 1995 so changed his name. He used to live with Casey in Doncaster but his real name was Angel Montseratte and it turned out that he was in fact a former professional in the States but was over here claiming 7lb in amateur-rider races. His riding style looked different gravy to the real amateurs in the Bollinger race series where he had a near-unbeatable lead until suspicions were raised and he got rumbled. He was given a ban of ten years.

FIFTY YEARS IN THE BETTING JUNGLE

Before then he also rode in an Arab race at Newmarket on Town Plate Day and his mount opened at 1/2 ON and drifted out to 2/1 against. Kevin was an on-course bookie that day and kept pushing him out and, you'll never guess what, he was very slowly away and finished second. When Angel returned to America having been banned over here, he was over the limit when involved in a car crash in which a teenager was killed and was sent to prison for ten years.

One of the shrewdest punters who I came across was Angus Hill who was the father of top point-to-point bookie Mark Hill. If any bookie made a rick, he would be first to step in to take advantage.

A punter who needs a mention is Norfolk's finest. No, not the turkey man but Olly West. A top-notch carpenter but an even better judge of a racehorse and I don't know how he does it but he always seems to find the winner of the lucky last. It's an uncanny knack that he possesses. Prince Monolulu was before my time but I would have loved to have seen him in action. Famous for his 'I Gotta Horse' shouts across the racecourse whilst wearing a head dress that would make Jamiroquai look embarrassed, although he described himself as the chief of an Abyssinian tribe, his real name was Peter Mackay which doesn't sound quite so exotic and he was married more often than Tammy Wynette claiming he had six wives during his life. I love my Country and Western but it always tickles me that her big hit was *Stand By Your Man*.

Even more so than wanting to see him in action, I would have loved to have taken him on in the betting ring. We would have made one hell of a double act as The Prince and the Pauper! Where have all the characters gone? His big win was Spion Kop at 100/6 in the 1920

Characters From The Betting Jungle

Derby where in today's money he won over £400,000. He choked to death on a strawberry cream according to the biography of Jeffrey Barnard who, when visiting him in hospital, left a box of Black Magic chocolates. What a way to go.

***

The Bookies.

I was making a book at Tweseldown when Pip Sims dropped dead on the pitch right next to me. He was in his eighties and would have wanted it no other way. He went doing what he loved. Pip was a pig farmer from Reading and a real character. Obviously octogenarian on-course bookmakers are very hard to find but we still have one in my mate David Bond who trades under the name of Cliff of Cambridge.

Brothers Alf and Harry White from King's Cross were other legendary point-to-point bookies. Harry's tipple was whisky and milk. He said the milk was good for him. Another from the old days pointing was Johnny Warren who was also from King's Cross but no relation to Bobby and Frank, who bet under J. Burrows.

Another London bookie was Dominic Sabini with his sidekick, Sausage, so called as he had a Butchers in Clerkenwell, and he bet under the name of Jack Remo. He also had a newspaper stand outside of Holborn tube station so used to sell papers first thing before heading to the races. Different times.

Walter Prince was a father and two sons' operation from Sarf London and were notorious for being late as the dad, Toffee, used to have a shellfish stall and wanted to make the most of those punters first.

FIFTY YEARS IN THE BETTING JUNGLE

Tony Colangelo of London changed his name to A Walsh of Reading as he thought that with a mafia-style name then no one would dare bet with him. I still see him at Cheltenham with his wife and he is now a punter.

The Falco brothers came from my neck of the woods, Islington, and all four had their own point-to-point pitches. There was Alf Collins (Mikey), Bingo (Terry), Parsons (Albie) and Billy (Ron Brazell). I only mention it as its unusual to have four bookies all from the same family.

Arthur Thomas aka Tommy Willey was from the same manor. He used to arrive early in his van to make all the wooden stands for the bookies so was known as The Woodman before he chalked up his board and took bets himself. We were going halves on the day at Mollington when Spartan Missile fell. His grandson, Ian Govey, runs the No.1 pitches at Huntingdon, Fakenham and Yarmouth and his grandad would have been proud of him.

Moving outside of the London bookies, Stoke-based Michael O'Rourke is a good pal who was a fellow bookie for about five years who bought a couple of Midlands pitches off me. He is now a novelist and his fourth and latest book was published just before Christmas called *Working Class Millionaires*. What I always aspired to be. A very interesting guy is Mick as he is also an antiques expert so is a regular at auction rooms all over the UK. I'm just waiting for his ugly mug to be seen on TV with Fiona Bruce. The only thing wrong with him is that he is a Chelsea supporter.

I wasn't big enough for The Sundance Kid himself, J P McManus, so Fearless Freddie Williams was his go-to bookie. Freddie had one leg shorter than the other due to a diseased pelvic bone that kept him

Characters From The Betting Jungle

out of school so he could barely read or write when he started off from a lowly shed in Ayrshire before being part of the Scottish greyhound circuit and went on to own a chain of shops. A businessman outside of bookmaking, he owned an Italian restaurant in Glasgow and set up a bottled drinks company in Cumnock where we used to stop off on the way up to Perth and he would give you his time, a bottle of water and a Tunnock's Teacake.

Back in 1998 when pitches first came up for sale at public auction, Freddie paid £90,000 for No.2 pitch at Cheltenham just four weeks after a triple heart bypass not helped by being a self-proclaimed seventy-a-day man. He famously lost almost £1 million in two races to J P at the 2006 Festival, made all the more famous as this was all caught on film for a TV documentary. That night he and his daughter Julie were ambushed by eight armed robbers in balaclavas who smashed the windows of his Jag and took the money satchel containing £70,000 in a back country road. Neither setback was going to stop Freddie though who returned the following Cheltenham. From humble beginnings he left a fortune of over £8 million. A true legend of the ring.

Dave Pipe was *the* legend of the West Country circuit who started off as a bookie at Butlins in Minehead. He was also a very successful sire but I never saw Martin at his pitch. I used to look up to him. Everyone did. He went from running a book from his home to selling forty betting shops to William Hill and even buying Martin a helicopter.

Also based in the South-West, I have mentioned Andy Smith earlier but this tale can't let go unreported. We were in the Royal Hotel after

FIFTY YEARS IN THE BETTING JUNGLE

Goodwood one night and we'd had a few. Andy spots an unmanned bus outside and with his brother asked if anyone fancied a ride up the sea front? No one answered but they still nicked the bus, drove it up and down the front and then left it on the other side of the pier. What I would have given to see the driver's reaction when he returned and found the bus on the opposite side of the road to where he had left it!

At Warwick I stood next to Barry Slaney whose clerk was a fresh-faced college kid who was the money finder, meaning that he would find the cash if Barry blew it. His name was Ben Keith who now takes the biggest bets in the ring under his Star Sports banner and proudly sponsors the Greyhound Derby.

Also from the Midlands, Bob Jacobs was a legendary Brummie bookie even though he spent more time in the bar than on his pitch.

The Asparagus Kid. Mickey Fletcher, was a staple of betting rings for decades having started off as a tic-tac and then a clerk. If you think that I can talk, then Mickey takes it to a different level so he is always a man that you could have a bit of fun with and he's got loads of stories. He used to buy asparagus from Birmingham Market off Matt Archer to sell it at the races and did so well that once a month he would have a week away abroad, often in Miami where he came back with boxes of King Charles Cigars which he could sell at ten times the price over here, until customs finally caught up with him. Mickey owned Kailash trained by Martin Pipe who became the first horse to win four bumpers.

When Kailash won Mickey used to give it to us bookies: "And there's another Louis Roederer Champagne and two fillet steaks for me and The Bomber." That was his pet name for his lovely wife,

Characters From The Betting Jungle

Angie. Mickey is now retired and goes away for the winter to places that I never knew even existed but he's always back for Cheltenham.

Mickey, Johnny Lights and me took our partners to the Royal Albert Hall but not before meeting up first for a late lunch at a swanky hotel. Mickey told us that it was good value so we got stuck into the carvery. Then the wine waiter reappeared after a while and said those feared words for men everywhere: "Are you okay for drinks, ladies?" We must have been watching a race on our phones in the bar or something as when we returned there were three bottles already half downed on the table. We didn't think anything of it until the old Beecham's Pill arrived and only then did we realise that they had bought the best Red in the gaff at £900 a pop so the bill came to £2,700! Good value you say? I've seen better value at Horseheath point-to-point in the 1980s.

When my youngest son Charlie was christened, we hired out a lovely venue in Knowle off the M42 and hired a top magician who was in his later years. Fletcher kept pouring him large whiskeys and he was blotto by the end of the service. Mickey's son then drove him mad during his show so he threw his cards in the air and buggered off. I've still got his wages if he wants them.

We lost Barry Dennis last year. To be honest I didn't have a lot to do with him but he did well to make a name for himself as he was very opinionated and knew how to play to the crowd. His 'Barry's Bismarcks' became a weekly feature on *The Morning Line* in his double act with Big Mac. He started out on the back row but with help from leading owner and fellow Romford boy David Johnson, he made it to the front row which multiplied his turnover seven-fold. I think it's fair to say that since he died, I have probably inherited the mantle of the most recognisable independent bookie in the ring.

Kettering bookie Roy Christie was a gentleman and was the main man at Yarmouth. On one occasion though, his car had broken down so I was the only bookie left on the rails. Roy had a regular local businessman who was a ten-grand-a-race punter so for that day his bets were placed with me. He lost on every race and never bet with me again. I must have been his unlucky charm.

Dudley Roberts bet on the rails but he was mainly a punter and had close ties to the Coolmore heirarchy so I was always looking at how he would play their runners.

Dan Hague was one the shrewdest layers I knew. On his board he had written 'The Man You Can Get On With' but I knew him as The Boston Strangler after where he came from and being the bee's knees on the East Anglian circuit.

I grew up with George Cooper aka Jamie Stephens and from day one he was fearless. If he had £5,000 in his pocket, he would give it a spin. There was no tomorrow as far as he was concerned. In a similar vein, Bert 'Battles' Rossi, also known as Bananas, was another character and when he won on the course, he would then give it a spin at the casino at night.

Michael Scotney never missed a day at Peterborough dogs until it closed down. Alongside his wife Audrey they were big supporters of the Marie Curie charity nights which I joined them for on a couple of occasions. We also both used to bet at trotting meetings, also known as harness racing, in Maldon on a Friday night. I did watch *Ben Hur* and fancied it myself but they didn't have a cart big enough for me.

Characters From The Betting Jungle

You need to have a different licence to bet in Ireland so I've never had a pitch there. I do love a day at Bellewstown though, where you are greeted at the gates by women selling oranges and Toblerone and their three-for-two offers. Midweek the attendances over there have plummeted so I'm struggling to see how some of the on-course bookies survive.

However, a new name doing well over there is Anthony Kaminskas who looks like the only new blood in the ring giving punters a crack of the whip. He came across as a shrewd punter over here and looks to have taken that with him setting up his online business AKBets. I met him at Cheltenham last year and he's one of us.

Another new name on the scene is Kalooki Bookmakers based in Ramsgate and they will take a big bet on course.

Come the Cheltenham Festival, Johnny Dineen used to travel over and was a pal in the betting ring. He was always in the front row whereas I was in the second row, and we had a friendly rivalry. He packed up being a bookie when the exchanges came into force to become a pro punter and has made a big name for himself since appearing on the *Upping The Ante* show and writing for *The Racing Post*. I've been on Cheltenham Preview nights with him at Uttoxeter and he has a great turn of phrase and sharp mind. Everyone loves a bit of Johnny.

Paddy Wilmott was another Irish bookie and punter that came over for Cheltenham. Given how hard he liked to enjoy a night out, it was odds-against that he would even turn up the next day but he somehow managed it. Johnny has said how much he learned from Paddy to the extent that if he had a fancy but

FIFTY YEARS IN THE BETTING JUNGLE

Paddy didn't like it, then that would dissuade him from having the bet. And me.

Ron Bolton was a big layer in the south who used to walk round with a bible. I don't know if he was looking for divine intervention or something but he was in the game for many years so, who knows, the Gods may have been looking after him in those photo finishes!

A E Thurston sometimes brought along his daughter Debbie who, if you asked her nicely, she would read your palm as she was from a travelling family. She still works on pitches today for Jay Rogers at the Eastern tracks and point-to-points. I could have done with her at Ascot one day.

Another 'A E' was A E Gardner from Southend-on-Sea. He only used to chalk up whole numbers on his board so no fractions like 13/8 or 9/4 and what have you. Strange but there you go, each to their own. Tanya Stevenson started out with Tony before her *Channel 4 Racing* days.

Laurie Bond of Eastbourne is one of the smartest bookies but never works on Saturdays being a massive Rangers fan so he has a season ticket and gets on the plane for all their home games.

Ex-pro cricketer Steve Wilkinson played for Somerset in the early-seventies and went on to have the No.1 rails pitch at Folkestone. His captain was Brian Close who told him: "You play too straight, lad." Funny that he went into being an on-course bookie then!

Not from the betting ring but Craig Reid is head of Betfred's traders and to my eyes he is one of the best judges in the racing game so I always ring him ahead of the big meetings. I knew him from the Tote

Characters From The Betting Jungle

days and when Betfred bought them, Craig went with him so it was the best free transfer since Sol Campbell from Spurs to Arsenal. A hell of a free transfer for Fred.

***

The Tic-Tacs.

I still yearn for the days of the tic-tac men and, believe me, there were few better than McCririck in his day. Codhead and Harold The Hat being two notable exceptions. The game needs them to help bring the betting ring back to life. The hundreds and thousands of pounds that went through their fingers.

The writing was on the wall for the tic-tacs in 1999 as just three were left plying their trade; Mickey 'Hokey' Stuart, Rocky Roberto and Billy Brown. It's actually Rocky that you see featured either side of the *ITV Racing* advert breaks. He later traded as Kel Ross but got out of the game.

Rocky is a fascinating character. Born of Italian descent, his dad was called Dante Roberto. Now, there can't be too many people who had two Derby winners as their name! So Rocky was always destined to work in the racing game. A softly-spoken man, he used to play cards on train journeys to the races, notably Epsom Downs.

Speaking of which, on Tattenham Corner there was a tic-tac called Winkle who only had one eye, which must have been razor sharp as he had to relay messages back and forth all the way to the grandstand. I doubt that even Steve Austin, the Six Million Dollar Man with his bionic eye, could have pulled that off.

The Midlands tic-tac Paul Doc was another top man at his trade and he loved a short one in-running before the advent of the exchanges.

FIFTY YEARS IN THE BETTING JUNGLE

We miss the reps on the course now as the 'Big Three' don't send them anymore as they have people sitting in front of screens shortening up horses instead. I got on best with Ladbrokes' Bobby Tellick. When I first started, he was the senior rep and took a liking to me. Also for The Magic Sign was Harry White and Niall Furlong. I seemed to get along with all the Ladbrokes reps.

If there were any disputes between bookie and punter, we dealt with the ring inspectors and most were ex-Scotland Yard. Andrew Boardley was ex-Flying Squad and a top bloke and is still in the game. They had a busy day when John Batten rolled into Epsom. Oddly enough, in half a century I don't think that I ever had a major dispute.

13
Dettori Day

The story has been told many times before but I still couldn't not include it could I?

If Queen always returned for an encore of *We Are The Champions*, ELO for *Mr Blue Sky* and Chas & Dave with *Ain't No Pleasing You* so, like with every good show, and I hope you think that the previous pages have been the literary equivalent, therefore so can Gary Wiltshire for an encore of the events of September 28th 1996 that made me. The old saying goes that you never see a poor bookie. Well, you saw a potless one that day.

Many of you will already be aware that I was on my way to Worcester but turned round to Ascot due to a traffic hold up around Banbury. Many of you will also be aware that I was a little in front for the day heading into the seventh and final race and that I arrived at the course with only £2,000 of what we call 'case money' but laid Fujiyama Crest to lose £1.4 million. So, let's go into the finer details a bit more than in the past.

Being back in the pre-internet days, on most Fridays I drove about one hour fifteen minutes down the M1 from near Milton Keynes into Kings Cross station to pick up *The Sporting Life* and *The Racing Post* to check out the runners and riders to help decide where we would be heading the following morning. They were usually bundled up at the newspaper kiosk and arrived by 9.45pm. It was either that or by *Ceefax* but I needed all the form and not just the runners and riders.

When looking through the cards for a couple of hours study-up when I got home at 11pm, I fancied getting a couple of the favourites beat at Worcester so the decision was made to head there the next morning before I hit the sack. I also had a pitch there but couldn't be 100% certain that we would pick up a spare one at Ascot. Once it was clear that we were in trouble arriving in time for Worcester, I said to Peter who was my clerk for the day, Ascot looks hard so let's head down there and see if we can make a day's wages of £300-£400.

You couldn't buy a pitch at Ascot for love nor money as they were handed down from father to son like season ticket holders at Anfield. If that sounds sexist, then I didn't mean it to be but pitches just weren't run by or owned by women except for one as Anthea Redfern, who was married to Bruce Forsyth, had one passed down to her by Frank Redfern of Torquay. They were a famous bookie family, there were loads of them. When the pitches came up for sale, Anthea was one of the first to sell up.

To get a pitch at Ascot I should have been at the course an hour before the first to see if there were any going spare. I arrived only fifty minutes before the first race but luckily, or so I thought at the time, two pitches were going spare at the end of the rails so I paid about a £70 pitch fee and made my way there in time to open a book for the first race. There were no boards on the rails those days, you just had to shout out loud, which I could do.

***

Dettori Day

On what is now the equivalent of Champions Day, the first four races came and went with no dramas for me personally even though the punters' favourite Frankie Dettori had won them all on Wall Street (2/1), Diffident (12/1) and Mark Of Esteem (100/30) for Saeed bin Suroor and Godolphin and Decorated Hero (7/1) for Johnny G. However, being the four televised races on BBC, the off-course firms had already done plenty on just the Yankees and Lucky 15s.

Knowing that Frankie was on the relatively-short-priced favourites in the fifth and sixth, the idea had already begun to circulate in my head exactly what I was going to do in the 'Lucky Last' if both Fatefully and Lochangel then won. And believe me, I was desperate that both would win as I saw this as my big chance, not just to win big but to win massive.

Fatefully then did the business as the 7/4 jolly giving Godolphin a four-timer and after Ian Balding's Lochangel made all to beat the other 5/4 jt-fav in the sprint I thought, this is it, this is my big opportunity. I was only a small bookie at the time but was hoping for that one chance to go for it and become a millionaire on the spot. If John Sullivan had written this script for Del Boy on *Only Fools And Horses* (how apt a title as it turned out) it was just too unbelievable a story line to take seriously.

By the way, without wanting to pour cold water on what was an incredible day for racing and Dettori, earlier on the card Lucayan Prince should have beaten Diffident on the snaffl! Watch it again and you'll agree with me, I guarantee it. The Choir Boy, Walter Swinburn, found all the trouble in the world on the second and would have won a minute with any kind of a clear passage as he was only done a short-nut and in front a stride after the line.

Not only that but there's also an argument that the aptly-named Fatefully should not have won the fifth race. Ray Cochrane found himself in a pocket for a furlong, held in by Frankie admittedly so good race riding, and was only beaten a neck so it could easily have been the 'Fantastic Five' or 'Super Six' rather than the 'Magnificent Seven' so fate(fully) certainly intervened that day. Literally in Cochrane and the horse's case.

Four years later and Cochrane saved Frankie's life following a plane crash in which the pilot died after which he received a Queen's Commendation for Bravery for extricating him out of the fire. He subsequently became Frankie's agent. Very sadly, Swinburn, the best big-race jockey that I have ever seen, died of head injuries at the age of just fifty-five having fallen out of his bathroom window.

So now it was six from six for Frankie and the firms had liabilities running into tens of millions. Stuff them, this was the chance that I had been waiting for all my life for to make it rich. In my mind, this was money for nothing.

I'd been doing alright though as had got myself three Mercs and a lovely house which Sandy Dudgeon, the Senior Steward of the Jockey Club up until last year, used to own and train from next to Little Horwood point-to-point course and the hugely-respected bloodstock agent James Delahooke was a nearby neighbour. James was best known for picking out Dancing Brave when a big part of Khalid Abdulla's racing empire but, with me being a point-to-point man, I best remember him for being the owner and trainer of Border

Dettori Day

Burg who won the Aintree Foxhunters'. How I bet they just loved having this loudmouth, lard-arse, cockney, bookie bringing down the reputation of the neighbourhood!

***

The final race was an eighteen-runner handicap over two miles and the Sir Michael Stoute-trained Fujiyama Crest was 16/1 in the morning for a good reason.

Being top weight, not only was he giving weight away to all seventeen rivals but he had lost his form having finished last but one in his previous race, the Northumberland Plate, so he had also been off the track for three months. In addition, on his last two runs they had resorted back to sticking on headgear. The only thing that I could see that he had going for him was having won the same handicap the previous year but he was 7lbs higher this time. Oh, and Frankie riding on a wave of confidence of course.

Having owned horses, I knew the only reason why they wore blinkers was because they were dodgepots in one way or another. Why else would you half blindfold a horse? So as a bookie I was always looking to lay them.

When I was interviewed on *Luck On Sunday* a few years back, I was making this very argument as part of my reasoning for getting stuck into Fujiyama Crest and asked: "How many horses can you name that have a won a Classic in blinkers?" For once Nick was stumped for a while before replying "not many" but came back with Secretariat and Northern Dancer in America but that's dirt racing where half of them wear blinkers anyway so I stand by it. What I will give Nick, however, is when he added: "But a few horses have won ordinary old handicaps at Ascot in blinkers though, Gary." I am told that interview was one my most watched on the show. Anyway, it was a visor and not a pair of blinkers but that's the same thing in my mind as it wasn't on for decoration.

And so it began. Whereas the other layers went 4/1, I shouted out 9/2. Ralph Leveridge of Coral wastes no time with £40,000 at 9/2. Bet. "What price Fujiyama now, Gal?" 4/1. "Twenty to win eighty." Bet. "What price now?" I shouted out 7/2. "Forty to win one-forty." Bet. I then took another fifty grand at 3/1. I was never going silly on the odds as was shouting just the next price up, only the amounts I was taking.

And then of all people Stephen Little asked for £20K to £55K at 11/4 at which point I asked: "What the hell are you doing, Stephen? You should be standing this!" He was known for cycling into work, so much so that he called his book *From Bicycle To Bentley*. I wanted to tell him to get 'on yer bike' but the bet was struck and then he just walked away. When I got round to paying him, he even charged me £4.60 for his stamped-addressed envelopes on his statements. He was a very good bookmaker.

I just couldn't stop myself and so it went on and on. Had the race been delayed five minutes I dread to think how much more I would have done. I wasn't financed by anyone as some have suggested, just playing with my own money.

The final odds I was shouting out was 2/1. These days the horse would have been nearer a Betfair SP of around 8/1. I was stood to win £660,000 if any of the seventeen horses could finish in

Dettori Day

front of Frankie Dettori and Fujiyama Crest and lose £1.4 million if they couldn't.

With history on the line *Grandstand* stayed on air but a commentator was needed as Sir Peter O'Sullevan had already downed a bottle of champagne so he wasn't in the fittest of states to accurately call an eighteen-runner race. He reportedly also hated doing races once his shift was over wanting to be well prepped. So the Beeb were on the lookout for another commentator on site and found John Hanmer who later said that he had also been drinking substantially with Sir Peter in the BBC Hospitality area once his shift as his spotter was over. As he was only half-cut though, he took on the responsibility.

I don't remember much of the race itself to be honest as I didn't know where I was. What I could see was that Frankie had set out to make all the running and was still in front when the quaint bell rang out as they rounded the final bend. It sounded more like a death knell to me that day.

There has been some chat since that the jockeys colluded to make sure that Frankie went through the card. I don't know how true that is, it seems unlikely to me, but that's the last thing that someone as competitive as Pat Eddery would have wanted and it was he was who was bearing down on Fujiyama Crest on Northern Fleet. When turning for home Richard Hughes said that Pat told him as he passed by that "He (Frankie) wouldn't be winning this one" and he was trying his hardest to catch him but came up short by a neck. The eleven-times champion also left us far too soon aged sixty-three following a heart attack.

FIFTY YEARS IN THE BETTING JUNGLE

If you read *The Racing Post* analysis on the race it's funny as there is not one single mention of Frankie winning all seven races! They concentrated instead that this race was a Cesarewitch trial and Fujiyama Crest wasn't even entered for it. Obviously they headlined on it elsewhere.

One of the big winners that day was Darren Yates which helped set him up in business and later as a racehorse owner and he won the Challow Hurdle with The New Lion. He had a £1 each-way accumulator and 50p Super Heinz on all seven winners totalling £62 with the betting tax pre-paid which saved him a pretty packet as he picked up £550,823.24 off William Hill.

Stories of other big winners started to flood in from small-punting Dettori fans. Fred Done gave all of his customers who won over £10K a video of the day's winners, champagne and cigars. Class. I had never spoken to Fred before but a few days later after I had been accused of costing the bookmaking industry an extra £10 million, he took time out to call me to say that I did absolutely nothing wrong and if he was in the same situation then he would have done exactly the same thing.

Mike Dillon of The Magic Sign went on to say that despite the huge losses, it was the best day that the bookmaking industry ever had.

Even after totting up the losses in the car park afterwards and then leaving the racecourse it didn't really hit me. That came the following afternoon. I was due to meet my Nicky at Milton Keynes dogs that night and didn't want to let him down but on the way I stopped off to see Ralph Peters in Amersham to tell him exactly what I had just done as needed to speak to somebody.

Dettori Day

Once I reached Milton Keynes ahead of the second race Nicky told me: "Dad, we've had a bad start, we lost £17 on the first." Little did he know! It was only half-way through the evening when I told him. When I got home that night to my house called *The Winning Post* in Towcester, the racing and local press were outside my house wanting the story and photos. I walked straight past them.

***

It was when I returned on the second day of the Ascot Meeting when the enormity of what I was facing really hit me. Sue Barker interviewed me on *Sunday Grandstand* and I just grinned and bared it. One well-known bookie was going round telling anyone willing to listen: "Don't bet with Wiltshire, he can't pay" so I never took a bet in five races and left. When I returned to my car, that's when it finally hit me slap bang in the face. I was the bookmaking equivalent of a leper, no one was going to touch me.

I have taken some good hidings in my time but never cried. There was no way I was going to give anyone that satisfaction. But I'll tell you one thing, I cried that day sat in the car wondering where do I go from here? The answer was straight to Loch Lomond and whilst there it even crossed my mind to end it all there and then as I could see no way out.

The following day I drove to the Coral office in Barking where their MD Trevor Beaumont couldn't have been more sympathetic and helpful. He asked me will I pay? I told him yes and he replied straight away: "You are a man of your word so that's all I need to know." I'll never forget it and how he stuck by me. Other firms would have preferred to take me to 'The Rooms'. Not like the back rooms in a Vegas casino if you were caught card counting back in the days when they were run by the mob but the term in this respect meant banning you as a bookie.

If I had walked away, then I would have got a ban and been back on the racecourse in a year. However, my name would have been dirt so I did the right thing.

Coral was extremely patient and after four years I had paid them back every single penny of the £487,500 that I was owing. William Hill wanted their £27,000 in a fortnight. That is fair enough, they were entitled to it, we can do that I thought, but not before I had paid out all the single punters first, none of which were cash bets, only credit.

Once they all got sorted, I went round four banks and drew all £27,000 out in one pound coins just to piss them off when handing it over, which I did to their racecourse rep in a service station on the A1 in two large satchels. Then I set about how I was going to pay back Coral and anyone else.

First to go was the three Mercs as no one I owed could see me driving about in any of my E320, convertible or jeep as that would have really stuck in their throat so they had to go, and go quickly. The villa in Portugal was next which I flogged for well under the odds but the big one was losing my home which I loved so that was a real kick in the nuts. They were all my assets of any worth so the rest of it had to come from long, hard graft. It may have taken me four years but I did it.

***

I have done various stunts with Frankie since, usually when celebrating a landmark of his incredible achievement so I dare say there might be another for the thirtieth anniversary next year!

Dettori Day

Outside of those, one time I was walking outside the Jumeirah Beach Hotel where the BBC put me up for the Dubai World Cup when some feller jumps up on my back and starts riding me like a horse shouting in his unmistakable accent: "Garrrry, Garrrry, Garrrry" and waving his right hand like he is about to whip me.

What an incredible person Frankie has been for the game since, the only name in racing to truly cut through to the general public since Lester Piggott and he is showing no signs of slowing up since his move to ride in America.

When I found out that Sotherby's were auctioning off Ascot memorabilia, there was no doubt in my mind, I just had to buy the 7th Race sign. It didn't matter how much it cost, it was going to be mine. Now it's in a box at Ascot as I gave it to my good friend, Mark Lowther.

So, what became of Fujiyama Crest? Well, the next time we saw him it wasn't for Stoute but Nicky Henderson! He had now got him to go hurdling with but won just once in six starts before being sent point-to-pointing where he pulled up in all three runs so clearly he didn't fancy that job. Following that he moved to Roger Curtis where he won just once in thirteen starts and that was in a claimer when rated a lowly 59 with the headgear taken off for a change. Told ya! When he was due to go through the sales ring, the Dettori Family bought him to live out his years at their home in Stetchworth.

One final footnote on all things Dettori Day, my son Charlie and his wife Bethany went on to call my grandson.... Frankie! Either they don't want me to forget his name for when I go senile or they have a very dark sense of humour!

14
These Days

I'm not brown bread yet. Far from it and you can also cancel the pipe and slippers as I get out and about as often as I can living life to the full and have racecourse pitches from Brighton to Perth.

These days I live in Melton Mowbray with my suffering partner of twelve years, Sharon. Don't worry I've heard all the jokes. That I only wanted to move closer to the pies. Who ate all the pies? Well, back in the day maybe but nowhere near so much now. In fact, I'm not even allowed on doctor's orders. A lovely lobster will do nicely, though.

***

Even though it's a round trip of over four hours, I never miss a Chelmsford Meeting if I can where I am the official bookie in the Owners' and Trainers' hospitality so we all know each other very well and I have made good friends there which you just can't buy.

John Holmes and his son Nathan do a fantastic job running the show some ten years on from when the racecourse reopened its doors. In my eyes it's a mini-Royal Ascot in that everything they do is done properly and the place is spotless. This is the Sport of Kings after all and Chelmsford treat you how you should be treated from the moment you pass the well-dressed security guards to leaving.

FIFTY YEARS IN THE BETTING JUNGLE

Pam Sharman runs all the betting operations at the course so it's nice to be working together with her again after our enjoyable years at the Tote, bar that one fateful day at York of course! She is also the part owner of L'Homme Presse.

***

It was not long after Nick Brereton had sold his medical company BresMed Health Solutions when I met him at Chelmsford where he had a horse called Oslo running and told me that he would love to get involved in the bookmaking business. Not realising at the time that he wanted me involved, I had to quickly backtrack after telling him that "the game's gone." The times I've told people that "the game's gone" since the advent of betting on mobile phones rather than looking into the whites of one another's eye, I've lost count. In fact, I gather I have developed a reputation for it!

Nick wanted to back his horse and I took £300 at 9/1. A minute later I had that £300 on at 11/1 on the exchange. When he came to collect, he felt genuinely bad until I showed him that I had backed it back so was up £600 myself so we were both happy.

From that point onwards we have enjoyed a great friendship and since his online BresBet operation was formed four years ago launching for the Covid Cheltenham Festival, I have been helping build the brand up for Nick and his wonderful family on the racecourse and through their social media platform. When BresBet become as big as Bet365, it's time for me to say goodbye to the racecourse but until then we'll keep punching away to make them a name to reckon with.

BresBet sponsor Fergal O'Brien's stable and the prestigious Easter Cup at Shelbourne Park and the Steel City Cup in Sheffield. In life

These Days

you meet bad people and genuine people and I can honestly say the Brereton's have been another lifer saver to me and my family.

***

Fred Done is another, literally on one occasion for which I will never be able to thank him enough. Once a month I appear on Betfred TV for their Sunday morning show to the shops from Media City as the studio guest. You've heard about the Oldest Swinger In Town, well meet the Oldest Pundit In Town and also the longest-standing for Betfred having appeared on their first Sunday morning broadcast which I still thoroughly enjoy appearing on.

Mark Pearson is Fred's right-hand man and leads the communications arm of the business having previously been Head of Programmes for Manchester United TV so he runs a very tight ship. Fred appears on some weekly shows and you will be amazed at how many punters turn up in the shops on Saturday mornings just to take advantage of 'Fred's Pushes'.

Betfred are sponsoring all five British Classics in 2025 and going forward including a £2 million Triple Crown bonus. Fred is not called The Bonus King for nothing! Their sponsorship portfolio also includes the British Masters at The Belfry which they have been supporting for the last seven years and they are also the official betting partners of Manchester United and Wembley Stadium. I could be here all day if listing all the other sporting events that Betfred proudly sponsor.

***

Although I can't bring myself to enter the Ascot betting ring again, I am happy enough quaffing their champagne and enjoying their smoked salmon in the hospitality boxes.

FIFTY YEARS IN THE BETTING JUNGLE

In fact, for Royal Ascot week I am the official bookmaker to the residents opposite the half-furlong marker on the inside of the course between the Royal Chalet and The Village. This is a spot reserved for just the locals, which is a nice touch from Nick Smith. And if called upon I have been known to have a racing story involving Ascot up my sleeve for anyone who asks! So I was delighted when Nick suggested that I be their resident bookie for the five days.

That week is not about money, it's a fun, pleasurable five days meeting old friends and *ITV Racing* sometimes come over to cover our little picnic area where their kids join us with their mums and dads after school.

***

My pitches remain spread all over the country and I try to put in an appearance on each of them at least once a year. The way the game has gone, the big festivals are the days that are going to determine if you have a winning or losing year.

I get punters coming up to me regularly asking for a winner in which case I always tell them to keep a close look out for Dusty Carpet the next time it runs as it will take a lot of beating. You'll be amazed how many times that gag goes over some heads!

I especially enjoy my trips to Scotland and the highlight of my last year was when my grandson Jack, when reaching the age of eighteen, helped me take bets at Perth and Ayr as he was at Uni in Glasgow. He only did one thing wrong. When a skinner in the book won one race, he was cheering it on like crazy and waving his arms in the air. You don't do that Jack, especially being a Wiltshire! He enjoyed it so much that, who knows, there might be another book in fifty

These Days

years' time! Jack's dad, Nicky, now lives in Troon so he is my licenced representative north of the border. I don't like to admit it but I think he's better than me.

On-course bookies are not gamblers anymore, just green-up merchants. With notable exceptions, and you know who you are, most of them don't have an opinion so are content being slaves to the betting exchange. If they can, they would be happy making a ton a day, seven days a week, twenty-eight days a month for around a three grand a month working wage.

Some of them love the student days with loads of kids basically not having a clue what they are doing so are rubbing their hands at the prospect but I purposely don't attend them. I don't want to take money off eighteen-year-olds. I know how gullible I was back then.

I still have pitches at point-to-points where my favourites are Kimble, Dingley, Ampton, Kingston Blount and High Easter. I do miss Hackwood Park, Tweseldown and Enfield Chase after their closing, though.

***

I still keep my hand in for a fun night at the dogs even if I haven't had a pitch at any track for over ten years now, all thanks to Mike Davis and his *Gone To The Dogs Live* shows on *YouTube*. I'm the betting pundit just like I was for Sky's greyhound coverage years ago before my operation and it's nice to see so many old faces.

I am still a straight and reverse forecast man. Always have been. Firstly, I look for a dog that will lead so missing all the trouble on the first bend. They may not always hang on but you're already ahead of the game. Then find a finisher. A dog that stays the distance very well and will be doing all its best work in the latter stages. They might not get there but I've got both a leader and a closer on my side and it is amazing how many reverse forecasts feature these kind of running styles.

***

I'm still the occasional bookmaker for Matchroom's darts and fishing when the big boys are not sponsoring the whole event. If you are reading this Eddie, although I love the Matchroom family, I don't fancy being on the boxing again after all the punches I take in jest. These days I bruise easily. I still see Barry and his wife occasionally at Chelmsford races.

***

I still love a bet but it's only recreational now. It's what keeps me going. The mental challenge. I don't know how I would occupy my mind otherwise. It's in my blood. I spend more time at the track than I do online and, believe it or not, I have not walked into a betting shop for four years.

When I lay a bet, I prefer to know who I am laying it to and look them in the eye. You have no idea who you are betting against on the machine. You could be taking on the owner or trainer or anyone else who is connected to a horse that has the edge over you. On the track I know exactly who I want to lay a chunky bet to and also who to gracefully knock back sometimes. It's called bookmakers' intuition and comes from years and years of experience.

It's also very hard to beat the exchanges, they *are* the market. If there are sixty bookies at Cheltenham and 75,000 playing on the machine,

These Days

then that's not sixty people setting the odds but 75,060. For those who do play on the exchanges, I would look at Betdaq closely. Their MD John Carthy and his brother Justin who is J P McManus' right-hand man and a Cheltenham Festival-winning owner are legends in the Irish bookmaking industry. Good people.

I actually think the Tote Placepot is the best bet as you can land big pots for small outlays and if you pick the right horses then it can give you an interest for the first six races. What's more you are not playing against a bookie as it's punters v punters and most of us fancy our chances in that situation. I remember the days of the Daily Tote Double on races three and five and the Treble on races two, four and six. I miss those bets.

***

On many occasions I have been asked to set up, join or put my name to a racing club but I have always turned it down. One day, maybe, when I am retired but I'm not planning that anytime soon! There is loads of life still left in the old dog yet.

I really hoped you enjoyed reading about my career in the betting game as much as I enjoyed putting it together. The Sport of Kings has been my life and given me the chance to meet so many legends, be it jockeys, trainers, owners, bookies or punters.

One thing I do want to say however is that being a bookmaker destroyed my personal life. I gave my children everything they needed except for the most important thing, Time. When I look back it hurts but that's too late now.

FIFTY YEARS IN THE BETTING JUNGLE

So that's it. Hopefully it's a long way off yet but you're all invited to the funeral where you can be guaranteed a rendition of *Together We'll Be Ok* by Cannon and Ball and enjoy some jellied eels. And where do I want my ashes spread for when I finally reach the great betting jungle in the sky? It's got to be Ascot. After all, I died there almost thirty years ago.